MIRACLE CHILD

*The Journey
of a Young Holocaust Survivor*

Anita Epstein
With Noel Epstein

Boston
2018

Library of Congress Cataloging-in-Publication Data:
The bibliographic data for this title is available from the Library of Congress.

Copyright © 2018 Academic Studies Press
All rights reserved.

ISBN 978-1-61811-858-5 (hardback)
ISBN 978-1-61811-859-2 (paperback)
ISBN 978-1-61811-860-8 (electronic)

Cover design by Ivan Grave.

Published by Academic Studies Press in 2018
28 Montfern Avenue
Brighton, MA 02135, USA
press@academicstudiespress.com
www.academicstudiespress.com

For our grandchildren,

Tessa, Jacob, Lilah, Max and Eli

Anyone who doesn't believe in miracles
is not a realist.

—David Ben-Gurion

Contents

Acknowledgments	8
Foreword by Michael Berenbaum	10
Introduction: Before It's Too Late	15

Part I: Origins

Chapter 1: In the Shadow of the Shoah	23
Chapter 2: Hotter Hells	34
Chapter 3: "Don't Let Her Take Me!"	49

Part II: Closed Doors

Chapter 4: New People, Old Problems	61
Chapter 5: Living With the Enemy	68
Chapter 6: In Search of Home	79

Part III: New World

Chapter 7: Becoming an American	93
Chapter 8: Falling for a Litvak	105
Chapter 9: Debts	113
Chapter 10: New York City Crisis and Beyond	121
Afterword	134

Acknowledgments

As with almost all authors, I owe a great deal to others, but I am of course solely responsible for any errors that may remain in this book.

As I need scarcely say, in addition to all else that I owe my mother and father, I incurred a large debt for the conversations we had over the years about the period covered by this work. But truth to tell my mother did not like to discuss specifics about the Holocaust, and I was extremely reluctant to "interview" her about everything that had happened. As a result, I am also indebted to the Shoah Foundation, housed today at the University of Southern California, for the interview the foundation did with my mother.

Others' knowledge and thoughts are also included in this work. When my mother and I visited Zofia Sendler in 1985, she explained what had happened while I was in hiding from the Nazis and when my mother found me again after the war. Her daughter Danuta also discussed these and other events with me. When we visited Lusia Avnon in Israel, she described what she recalled about the arduous post-war trip with my mother from Bergen-Belsen to Krakow, and her self-published book on her life was helpful on this and other scores. In New York, her sister Helga offered her thoughts as well, particularly about life in Selb, Germany.

Among family members, my other largest debt is to my husband, who has been keeping notes on my life for years and whose research and writing skills have been critical, especially since I began suffering several years ago from serious illnesses.

In addition, my late cousin Paul Rolnicki reviewed with me the days when his father and mine were in the Soviet military, my cousin Inka Hauser provided her insights as well, and my sister-in-law Helene Kaminski gave me valuable advice.

I am also grateful to family members who critiqued the entire manuscript at various stages, including my daughters Stephanie and Pamela and my cousin Sally Koslow, a talented author who introduced me to the New York Writer's Workshop, where I received an array of helpful comments.

In addition, Michael Berenbaum, Henry Waxman, Stuart Eizenstat and Henryk Grynberg all read the entire manuscript and offered varied thoughts, including those Prof. Berenbaum generously penned in his forward and the kind assessments that Messrs. Waxman, Eizenstat and Grynberg provided for the book's back cover.

Finally, I can never repay all the historians, attorneys, journalists, documentarians, Holocaust victims and others whose writings and films on the Holocaust and related issues inform this work. I hope that I have done them justice, that the book does not fall too far short in depicting the madness that was the Shoah.

Foreword

"Now it's my turn."

With these words Anita Epstein assumes her rightful role as a child survivor of the Holocaust, one who knows that she and other Jewish children who escaped death during the Shoah will be the last survivors. After they go the way of all flesh, the Holocaust will move from living history to historical memory; the content of that memory will be different, as will its ethos.

Children of her generation—and of mine—were always taught to wait their turn. Anita did so respectfully, understanding that while her mother was alive her story was central, Anita's but an embellishment. Some child survivors were less respectful, and their parents often belittled their children's memories, saying, "What could you know—you were only a child. What can you remember—you were so young." And because Anita was in hiding and not in the camps, her unique testimony was negated even more. Her suffering and her loss, real as they were for her, were secondary to the terrible tragedies of the adults who had been in the ghettos and camps. Thus, sometimes without thinking and certainly without understanding the cruel effect of their statements, ghetto and camp survivors were dismissive of the children and of others who lived in hiding, whether by passing as non-Jews or living in clandestine hiding places.

Yet now, more than three score and ten after the liberation of Auschwitz, child survivors' testimonies become all the more

Foreword

important, for they will delay the inevitable transition, and the memory of the Holocaust will be enriched as a result.

Okay. It's her turn, and Anita Epstein has quite a story to tell.

She was conceived in love, perhaps in a flash of abandon that happens between husband and wife when, for a moment, all that matters is their love. No one who pondered the ghastly conditions of the Krakow ghetto in 1942 would have contemplated bringing another Jewish child into that world. And yet, a child was born there—Anna Künstler. Obviously, given the circumstances of her birth, there was no birth certificate. Were the birth to have been registered, her birth certificate also would have been her death certificate.

Such a child was not expected to live. Only one in ten of all Polish Jews survived the Holocaust, and the number was lower for Krakow, where Jews were deported to the death camps of Auschwitz and Belzec and where the "neighborhood" camp of Plaszów, under the cruel commandant Amon Goeth, was less than two kilometers away. And yet she did live.

We read of her rescuer, Zophia Sendler, who provided scarce food and desperately needed shelter to the young girl during the war. In Israel such women are called "Righteous Among the Nations of the Earth," but such an exalted status describes neither the simplicity of the deed and its majesty nor its motivation. Zophia was a religious woman; although she was promised recompense after the war, a share in a lovely home and some wealth, her religion was not one that permitted her *not* to offer a haven to a child condemned to die, even if such a child was a Jew. At considerable risk to herself and her family, she took in the baby girl and raised her alongside her own children. All the while, elsewhere throughout German-occupied Poland, other Jewish children were being murdered—"exterminated" was the word that the Germans used— and Poles who saved some of them similarly risked not only their own lives but those of their families as well. Still, the atmosphere in the Sendler family was not all peace and tranquility. Zophia's husband, who must also have consented to offering shelter, was an abusive, wife-beating man. In the scope of things, this merits little mention, as it is overshadowed by all else. In her rescue home Anna Künstler became Anya Kasperkevitch; a Jewish infant became a Roman Catholic.

Zofia Sendler was by no means Anita's sole savior. As Epstein learned, she owed a great deal to the father she cannot remember, to his quick thinking to sedate her and give her away, escaping the liquidation of the Krakow ghetto, taking a taxi to hand off his daughter, and then courageously returning to the ghetto to be with his wife, come what may. In one paragraph, we see the wisdom, courage and forethought of her later-murdered father. Survival required all three characteristics—and, above all, luck.

If Epstein were writing a Hollywood script, she would have depicted the reunion with her mother, a survivor of Auschwitz and Bergen-Belsen and other camps, in all its glory: mother and daughter are reunited, the bond reestablished at once, and off they go into the sunset. Why spoil the actual drama by foretelling the event? Suffice it to say that her mother, Eda Künstler, was wise enough to restrain herself and not to impose her needs upon the child, and Zofia was so very decent that she enabled the transition between the biological mother and the only mother Anya knew, her foster mother, to go as smoothly as possible.

As a little girl who survived what later became known as the Holocaust, Anna was regarded as a "miracle child." For adult survivors who witnessed so much death, the presence of this young child, the embodiment of life, was deeply cherished. In 1945, there were almost no Jewish children left in their world. Only after survivors married each other—frequently out of desperation and loneliness—and had children, often because women who had ceased menstruation in the camps were afraid that they would never conceive, were there other Jewish children around. Until

Foreword

then, Anna was the only child, the cherished child, the beloved child.

Twice in this book I was bemused by coincidences, juxtapositions of her life and mine. Anita took a screen test to play Anne Frank in George Stevens' classic rendition of *The Diary of Anne Frank*. She may not have been chosen for the role for various reasons, including that she looked too Jewish. In the 1950s, after all, it was a handicap to be "too Jewish," especially if a film studio and a director were seeking to create a universal story. It might also have been because they feared that Anita's own Holocaust story might have overshadowed Anne's, in which the Holocaust is only dimly in the distance. Anne begins her "Holocaust" experience only after her diary ends, when there is the knock at the door. One wonders if some of the criticism of the false universalization of *Diary* might have been the same had an actual survivor played the role.

Anita also shares an annoyance with Eva Kor, who with her twin sister was a victim of Dr. Joseph Mengele's ghastly "experiments" at Auschwitz. Kor suddenly decided in the 1990s that she could forgive the "Angel of Death" and other Nazis and thereby make peace with her Holocaust experience. Having assumed the role of the heavy in the film *Forgiving Dr. Mengele*, I joined in Anita's opposition to such "cheap grace." Even though she is a survivor, Kor is not the one who can offer forgiveness and certainly not if it has not been earned by acknowledgment, confession, and resolve, the three essentials of repentance, the minimum requirement for forgiveness.

The sense of the miraculous survivor seems to have given Anita a character of strength and a resilience that has accompanied her through life. I will restrain myself from commenting on her immigration and Americanization—she does that with grace, humor and gratitude—and having known Anita and her husband Noel for so many years, I can only say that by reading this memoir I learned much about two people I thought I knew, and so will you.

Foreword

Though you will read many sad things in this book, this is not a sad book but a powerful work by an accomplished woman, self-confident and ready to take center stage in service of memory. Now that it is her turn, we must celebrate how much she has to say, the depth and the power of her memory.

Michael Berenbaum
American Jewish University
Los Angeles, California

Introduction
Before It's Too Late

In 1995, when she was nearly 80 years old, my mother was interviewed by the Shoah Foundation about her ordeals during the Holocaust—the torments of Hitler's camps, including Auschwitz and Bergen-Belsen, the murders of almost all her family members, the recurring anxiety about whether her baby girl, who had been hidden from the Nazis, was still alive. Near the end of the interview, she was asked whether she wanted to impart any thoughts to her children and grandchildren. Her first answer was simple and direct: "Not to forget."

While the Holocaust will never be entirely forgotten, survivors worry that the public will pay less and less attention to it as it recedes further into history. That is certainly the case for many in my generation; we were the children then (I was the little girl who was hidden), and before long we will be the last remaining survivors. After us there will no longer be any who lived through it, none telling their tales at the world's Holocaust museums, none speaking to classrooms, none lighting candles at memorial services on *Yom Ha'Shoah* (Holocaust Remembrance Day).

Granted, second- and third-generation groups, museums, synagogues, schools, publishers, film producers and others will continue to spread knowledge of the Shoah after we are gone. Their task, though, will be more challenging. For one thing, post-survivor voices obviously will not carry the same weight as those who spent their days clinging to life in camps amid gassings, burnings,

15

beatings, shootings and hangings, those who starved, froze or collapsed from exhaustion or disease, those who lived in disguise or in hiding and in constant fear of being discovered. Those are the voices—Primo Levy, Elie Wiesel, Anne Frank and others—that moved the world. For another thing, Americans unfortunately set no great store by history, whether of their own country or the world. Indeed, one survey of Holocaust knowledge found that of seven nations examined—the United States, Germany, France, Great Britain, Austria, Poland, and Sweden—Americans knew the least about the subject. Most Americans could not even identify Auschwitz as a concentration camp.

In addition, post-survivor voices will have to counter the increased cheapening of words like "Holocaust," "Hitler" and "Nazis." Various political advocates cannot seem to stop hurling "holocaust" at their target of the week. In 2004, for example, an animal-rights group sponsored a traveling exhibit called the "Holocaust on Your Plate"; its large photographs equated a stack of pig carcasses with piles of human corpses and otherwise compared concentration camp victims with animals. Others speak of an "abortion holocaust," an "environmental holocaust," a "tobacco holocaust," or they hurl "Nazi" or "Hitler" regularly at opponents (especially, perversely, when they are Palestinians attacking Israelis). True, corruption of these words is not new. Nearly 30 years ago Nobel Peace Prize winner Elie Wiesel lamented the use of "holocaust" in the media to describe the drubbing of a sports team or the murder of half a dozen people. Since then, however, the trivialization of these words has multiplied many times over. In fact, calling someone a "Nazi" online has become so commonplace that the phenomenon has given birth to "Godwin's Law," an adage created by one Michael Godwin and defined as follows by the Oxford English Dictionary: "the theory that as an online discussion progresses, it becomes inevitable that someone or something will eventually be compared to Adolf Hitler or the Nazis, regardless of the original topic."

16

Before It's Too Late

All this, of course, is to say nothing of those who preach that the Shoah never happened, that there were no gas chambers at Auschwitz-Birkenau or that Anne Frank's diary was a forgery. Yes, the Holocaust deniers are, at least in the United States, a relatively small fringe group (in other lands, especially among Muslim communities and particularly in the Middle East and North Africa, they are, sadly, far more plentiful). Yet if we have learned anything from the Nazis and the Holocaust it is the peril of not taking fringe groups seriously enough, especially since this particular group is spewing more and more of its lunacy onto the Internet. Thus, the world must be reminded repeatedly that the Holocaust not only happened but that it was the height of human horror. People need to understand that "Holocaust" is not synonymous with "disaster," "mistreatment," "catastrophe" or large numbers of deaths, that it was savagery on a unique scale, the ultimate evil.

Perhaps the largest challenge to keeping the memory of the Holocaust alive, though, will remain that staggering number: 6 million. Who can wrap their mind around that magnitude of madness? Who can summon the ocean of tears needed to cry for 6 million murdered Jews? Who can imagine the faces of the 1 million to 1.5 million children among the piles of corpses? Sometimes I try, especially when I think of how close I came to being one of them. The mind-boggling number, though, keeps getting in the way. That is why we survivors have to tell our tales: in the hope that our personal stories can help the next generation and generations to come better grasp the horrors inflicted on millions and to explain how the relatively few of us who did not perish fared in our lives. In addition, we need to keep beating the drums against the new Jew-hatred that has emerged, especially in the Middle East and Europe.

My own story has its share of tragedy, but I certainly do not view myself as a tragic figure. After all, I was among the tiny fraction of Jewish children in Poland—a mere one-half of one percent—who emerged from the Holocaust alive. I also have a great deal to be

17

thankful for. My mother and first father, who died in Mauthausen, saved me from the crematoriums. Remarkably, my mother, though terribly ill after the war, still managed to travel for weeks and find me again. My second father, who survived Stalin's Siberia and killed Germans on the eastern front as a member of the Red Army, was an unwavering pillar of strength and support and love. My husband, two daughters, two sons-in-law and five grandchildren, as well as my brother and his wife and children, all bring me great joy. We clearly outwitted the Nazis by multiplying again.

But there were trying times along the way. At war's end, when my mother tracked me down after she had survived four of Hitler's camps, I was torn screaming from the Polish Catholic family where I had been hidden, a family with whose last surviving member I am still in touch. When my mother and I became what were euphemistically called "Displaced Persons" (DPs), anti-Semitism was rife in U.S. DP camps in Germany. One need only recall the vile remarks of U.S. General George Patton, then Military Governor of Bavaria, who saw Jewish DPs as "lower than animals" and treated them accordingly. Indeed, President Harry S Truman's envoy to U.S. DP camps reported after a 1945 inspection tour that "we appear to be treating the Jews as the Nazis treated them except that we do not exterminate them."

We lived at that time in Selb, in Bavaria, birthplace of the Nazi party, while we and everyone else we knew searched for someplace else to go, for someone to open a door for us. We spent eight months in Great Britain with my mother's sole surviving sister, who had wed in England before the war, but the United Kingdom was not high on my mother's list of possible new homes. Post-war England, after all, was one of many countries with a continued aversion to Jews. It excluded Jewish DPs from the lists of East Europeans it imported to work in its coal mines, its steel and textile mills and other parts of its wobbly economy, and, of course, it had sought to placate Arab leaders by reneging on its support for a Jewish homeland and

Before It's Too Late

restricting Jewish entry into British-controlled Palestine. Many Jews reviled Britain for this, especially after its heartless treatment of survivors on the *Exodus 1947*, the Palestine-bound ship it rammed and boarded off the coast of Haifa, killing or maiming a number of DPs who resisted the boarding party and sending thousands back to camps in Germany. At the same time, much to my mother's frustration, U.S. anti-Semitism kept America's doors closed as well. In the end, however, with some maneuvering around a new anti-Jewish immigration law in America, we finally managed to make it to Ellis Island in late 1949, when I was 7 years old.

New York immigrant life in the 1950s also had its struggles. With little money, we lived in another ghetto, Brooklyn's Bedford-Stuyvesant. For entertainment, kids there sometimes played a game called "Hit the Rat," in which we would swing sticks at rats in the streets and try to chase them into sewer drains. In our apartment at 268 Pulaski Street, we would hold up our feet while mice went by our chairs. In elementary school I was placed initially in a class for "the retarded" (today's "intellectually disabled") simply because I did not yet have a full command of English, and in junior high school I ended up during recess one day with classmates throwing two darts in my back. In addition, a girl named Henrietta, who headed a Brooklyn gang called the Lady Chaplains, threatened me and told me to meet her and her friends after school. I did, but I told her that I didn't understand why she wanted to meet. She said to fight, of course. I asked why I would want to fight. She said I must be joking. I told her that I wasn't. Evidently thinking that I was either an imbecile or insane, she decided to become my protector. From then on, every weekday during the school year she walked me to junior high school in the morning and back home again in the afternoon.

I didn't tell Henrietta about my history during the Holocaust and rarely mentioned it to other children. Most didn't know what the Holocaust was anyway. As for the few who did, if I tried to explain

19

my story they either looked at me in a peculiar way, as if I were different (which I hated), or they asked uncomfortable questions. The one I disliked most was whether I had nightmares. Yes, I had nightmares, mostly about being chased and running as fast as I could to escape, and I frequently awoke screaming. But I disliked talking about that. Besides, I had spent some time deliberately not saying anything to my mother about my sleep demons. With everything she had been through, after all, how could I complain about frightening dreams, particularly since she suffered from far more horrible nightmares? Okay, I did tell my mother once about a nightmare, but I stopped after she dismissed it by saying, once more, that I had never been in the *lager* (the concentration camp) and that the bad dreams would go away. They never did. They are much less frequent now, but at times I still scream in my sleep.

Of course, there were pleasant experiences as well. I had some wonderful teachers, for example, including one in junior high who conspired to keep me away from an awful neighborhood high school and to enroll me in a better one further from home, Thomas Jefferson High. There I became "Miss Jefferson," wrote an advice column for the school paper, and did well academically. During those high school years, moreover, Academy Award-winning film director George Stevens gave me a screen test and auditioned me twice for the part of Anne Frank in his 1959 movie version of *The Diary of Anne Frank* (why I didn't get the role is an interesting question that will be explored later). As an adult, I quit my job teaching English to foreigners in Washington (where my husband was working for *The Washington Post*) and, without pay, created a group that helped, at least modestly, to stave off bankruptcy for New York City, which had opened its arms to so many immigrants like me. Although forgoing my salary squeezed our budget, I felt compelled to help the city secure federal loan guarantees during its 1970s fiscal crisis, when New York temporarily lost its borrowing power in the bond markets. As a result of that experience, I ended up becoming a lobbyist, first for the nation's state boards of education and later for Mexico and other international trade clients, pushing laws, regulations and national policies in Washington instead of *schmatas* in Manhattan.

Although my adult life has been filled with a wonderful family and dear friends and colleagues, I long had a nagging sense of being left out, of not fully belonging, because I was neither a concentration camp survivor (thank goodness) nor a second-generation offspring born after the war. Beyond a scattered friend or two, I knew nobody with a similar history. It was a great comfort to me, therefore, to discover a group in the Washington area, now called "Survivors of the Holocaust—The Last Generation," which meets monthly at one of our homes and which is part of a worldwide federation of child survivors. As I listen to other members' stories and deal with the issues we all face, I know I am no longer alone.

I have waited a long time before putting any of this to paper. Partly this was because remembering the past has sometimes been painful. Partly it was because placing the story in historical context—which I consider essential if the young are to have any chance of understanding what happened—took me some time. Most of all, however, it was because I could not get myself to write a memoir while my parents were still alive and able to tell their own tales. I would wait my turn. My parents, after all, are the ones who suffered far more than I did and who began all over again with little more than memories of a broken world left behind them. They were the remarkably resilient ones, living on little in a foreign land, in a foreign language, with foreign customs and nonetheless succeeding. They are the ones to whom I owe everything. May they rest in peace (זצ"ל).

Now it's my turn.

Part I

Origins

Chapter 1
In the Shadow of the Shoah

A thousand years will pass and still this guilt
of Germany will not have been erased.
*—Hans Frank, Hitler's Governor-General
of Poland, who was hanged at Nuremberg*

I stood in front of the exhibit at the U.S. Holocaust Memorial
Museum in Washington, D.C., struggling to control my tears. The
exhibit was called "Life in Shadows: Hidden Children and the
Holocaust." In one glass case was an old photograph of my mother
in a white blouse, looking like a schoolgirl. Next to the picture was
a letter she had written from Poland's Krakow ghetto, in early 1943,
to the Catholic family outside that she prayed would hide me. My
mother implored the wife, Zofia Sendler, who had three children of
her own, to have pity on her three-month-old daughter, to save me
from the Nazi slaughter.

The Nazis, it hardly needs saying, harbored paranoid fantasies
about Jews wielding astounding power—enough to cause
Germany's defeat in World War I, to create German hyperinflation
in the early 1920s, to manipulate both capitalism and communism
(Nazis liked to call it "Judeo-Bolshevism"), even to plot to control
the entire world. This was all news to the Jews, of course, but
ridding society of Jews for these and other reasons was gospel to
the Nazis. After all, the Fuehrer had written in a 1919 letter about
the need for "the irrevocable removal of the Jews" from German

23

life, and he had declared in a 1922 interview, "Once I really am in power, my first and foremost task will be the annihilation of the Jews." Lest anyone think that Hitler's anti-Semitic ravings were not evident before the two volumes of *Mein Kampf* were published in 1925 and 1926 and certainly long before the Holocaust began, he raged in that interview:

> As soon as I have the power.... I will have gallows built in rows– in the Marienplatz in Munich, for example—as many as traffic allows. Then the Jews will be hanged indiscriminately, and they will remain hanged until they stink; they will hang there as long as the principles of hygiene permit. As soon as they have been untied the next batch will be strung up, and so on down the line, until the last Jew in Munich has been exterminated. Other cities will follow suit, precisely in this fashion, until all Germany has been completely cleansed of Jews.*

During World War II, however, Hitler first had to deal with another problem: severe worker shortages at home and in conquered territories. He sorely needed millions of slave laborers to plow fields and produce weapons, mine quarries and make clothes, and able-bodied Jews were among the many who could do this work. Deliberately keeping Jews alive for whatever purposes was, naturally, a troubling concept for some Nazis, but they quickly solved their dilemma: Jews fit for labor, they decided, would literally be worked to death, a policy known as *Vernichtung durch Arbeit* ("extermination through work"). This pleased not only the SS but also German industrialists and mine owners, who were eager for cheap prisoner labor provided by the SS, as well as worried German food planners, who knew that toiling Jews would get exceedingly meager rations, barely enough to stay alive, if that.

---

* Quoted by Gerald Fleming in *Hitler and the Final Solution* (Berkeley, CA, and Los Angeles, CA: University of California Press, 1984), 17.

Chapter 1. In the Shadow of the Shoah

Other Jews, though, were not to be spared, even temporarily. The elderly? They were of no value. The sickly? Just burdens who required doctors, nurses and medicines needed at the front. The young children? Useless nuisances who would grow up to seek revenge while repopulating the world with Jews. So along with various Jewish leaders and any pregnant Jewish women they could find, the Nazis killed the old, the ill and the young. Not long before my mother wrote her letter to Zofia Sendler, for example, SS troops in the Krakow ghetto shot and killed 300 Jewish orphans as well as hundreds of Jewish hospital patients and old-age home residents. The Germans especially seemed to relish murdering the young, not just by shooting them but also by grabbing babies by the feet and cracking their skulls against walls, throwing children out of upper-story windows, using them for target practice, or burning them alive. As a result, up to 1.5 million Jewish children in Nazi-occupied lands in Europe died in the Holocaust; only one in 10 survived. For Poland, where I was hidden, the numbers were far worse: of the one million Jewish children in Poland in 1939, when Hitler invaded to start World War II, a mere one-half of one percent escaped death. That's why, when Poland survivors saw me after the war, a number of them called me the "miracle child."

I have often wondered why I was spared, whether it was mere luck or part of some grand design, whether I was required to achieve something extraordinary in life, to become someone special, to justify my continued existence. If so, I clearly have fallen far short. At the same time, in light of the starvation and disease and corpses and stench in the streets of the packed Krakow ghetto, I have also wondered what on earth my parents were thinking when they conceived me there. I have to assume that they were still intoxicated with love and that thinking had absolutely nothing to do with it.

When they met, my father, Salek Künstler, was the aristocratic-looking third son of a well-to-do Krakow family that liked to vacation

25

55 miles south in the Carpathian Mountains, in Zakopane, Europe's largest ski resort north of the Alps. My mother, Eda Dükler, who enjoyed skiing and horseback riding and hiking, was the third of five daughters of a general-store owner, a religious man of modest means, in the Carpathian village of Zawoja. My parents met in the Carpathians, courted in Krakow, where my mother had found work as a bookkeeper, and wed there on August 30, 1939, when my father was 25 and my mother 23. That would not seem to say much for their timing: Two days later, on September 1, the German blitzkrieg began its thrust across Poland. However, forebodings of war had long been in the air, and my parents, I am told, wanted to marry before the fighting broke out.

Almost immediately after the invasion of Poland, the Nazi abominations began. In many cases, the mobile SS death squads in the invasion's rear set fire to synagogues, burning Jews inside and shooting those who fled the flames. In other cases, Hitler's henchmen engaged in such obscene acts as performing a gynecological exam to search for jewels while looting a Jewish home, setting fire to a rabbi clutching a holy Torah scroll, or tormenting crippled or blind Jews for amusement. Mostly, though, they simply rounded up Jews and shot or hung them, heaving their bodies into mass graves that they often had forced their victims to dig for themselves. As Martin Gilbert notes in *The Holocaust: A History of the Jews of Europe During the Second World War*, "In the first 55 days of the German conquest and occupation of Western and Central Poland 5,000 Jews were murdered behind the lines: dragged from their homes, and from their hiding places."

That killing pace, however, frustrated the SS, which found it impossible to get rid of Jews quickly enough for its liking. At a rate of 5,000 every 55 days, after all, it would take more than 30 years to kill a million Jews—and the Nazis now had far more Jews on their hands than that. In Germany the Jewish population in 1933, when Hitler came to power, had been little more than 500,000, and it was

Chapter 1. In the Shadow of the Shoah

possible then for the Nazis to advocate Jewish emigration (and to gloat when virtually the entire world, including the United States, refused to accept desperate Jewish refugees). Poland, however, was home to about seven times that number, or about 3.5 million Jews, more than 2 million of whom came immediately under German rule. How on earth could the Nazis shoot, stab, strangle, suffocate, burn, bayonet, behead or otherwise butcher 2 million Jews? How could they spare the manpower, the ammunition, the time?

It was questions like these that led the Nazis to pollute the Polish landscape with gas chambers and crematoriums at Auschwitz, Belzec, Treblinka, Chelmno, Sobibor and Majdanek. Just three weeks after the invasion of Poland, the *Einsatzgruppen*—those special SS death squads—also had received orders from Berlin to begin corralling Jews together in larger cities, separate from the rest of the population and near a rail line, which was to prove useful later in transporting them to killing camps. Although it took longer than the Nazis had anticipated to create these ghettoes, in Krakow as elsewhere the SS, Gestapo and German police marched relentlessly toward that goal:

- THE IMPORTANCE OF LOOTING. In October 1939, Jewish homes, including that of my father's family, were looted for whatever valuables and currencies could be found. Such looting was vital to Hitler's prosecution of the war. Stolen Jewish assets, after all, financed about 30 percent of Germany's military at one point, as a 2010 study for the German Ministry of Finance showed. A curfew also was imposed that month; any Jew in Krakow's streets or on a balcony after the curfew was shot on sight.

- SEIZING HOMES AND BUSINESSES. In January 1940, Jews were required to register their premises and enterprises, which the Nazis later distributed to Germans, Poles or Western Ukrainians. Thus my father's family lost both their large leather company and their four-story home in the center of Krakow, at Ujejskiego Street 13.

27

Part I. Origins

- CREATING THE 'CLEANEST CITY.' In April 1940, the Nazis ominously declared that Krakow—which Hitler had made the capital of the new General Government for unannexed Polish territory and which Hans Frank, former general counsel of the Nazi Party, now headed as Governor-General—would be the "cleanest" city in the regime, meaning that it would be rid of all Jews.

- EXPELLING THE JEWS. In May 1940, the Germans started pressuring Jews to leave the city "voluntarily." By mid-August 1940, however, they were unhappy with the results and began expelling Jews themselves to other cities and villages. By March 1941, nearly a year later, about 55,000 Jews had been resettled.

- CRAMMING THE REST INTO 15 STREETS. In March 1941, the Nazis finally succeeded in creating the Krakow ghetto, with the remaining 15,000 Jews in the city ordered to live there by March 20. This "Jewish living quarter" was in Podgorze, which had not been a Jewish neighborhood before but was within easy walking distance of a train station. With just 15 streets and little more than 300 mostly shabby buildings, the ghetto had been home to 3,000 residents before the war. Now, enclosed by a wall with tombstone-like arched tops as well as by barbed wire, its apartments had to house five times that number, creating severe over crowding.

Initially, my parents were not among the Krakow ghetto dwellers. Like nearly 100,000 other Polish Jews in 1939, they had fled east from the Germans to Lemberg (now Lvov, in today's Ukraine), which Stalin had swiftly taken over under the infamous German-Soviet Non-Aggression Pact. Misery under the Soviets, even deportation to Siberia, as happened in thousands of cases, was preferable to likely death under the Nazis. Nineteen months later, in June 1941, however, Hitler attacked along a broad front in the east, breaking his unholy alliance with Stalin, who was not accustomed to dealing with a leader who was even less trustworthy than himself. Jews in Lemberg and elsewhere in Soviet territory trembled again. They feared death at the hand of the Germans or the Ukrainians (who were

Chapter 1. In the Shadow of the Shoah

in fact to murder several thousand Lemberg Jews in horrid pogroms) or of ending up in a concentration camp or another ghetto (which the Nazis indeed created and quickly filled in Lemberg, though not before shooting thousands of old and sick Jews on their way to its gates). Some Jews tried to hide. Others fled further east, again to outrun the Germans.

My parents had not decided what to do when two SS men from Krakow showed up looking for them in Lemberg. My grandparents had bribed the SS men to drive my father and mother the 200 miles back to Krakow, so they could at least be with the rest of their family. That settled the question: My parents would return. When they did, my mother and father were squeezed into the three-month-old Krakow ghetto, living in a single room with three other families. I have never known their names.

At the time of their arrival in Krakow, a good number of ghetto residents still were struggling to maintain a semblance of normal life. They lit Shabbat candles on Friday nights, sent children to secret classes with ghetto teachers, arranged occasional marriages, kept forbidden diaries, and sang such popular Yiddish songs as *Es Brent* ("It's Burning") by the poet Mordechai Gebirtig (who lived and died among them in the Krakow ghetto). But the brutal Nazis policies quickly made life anything but normal. Food grew scarce. Beggars in rags became commonplace, as did starvation. Skeletal corpses or near-corpses littered the streets. Garbage piled up. Rats were plentiful, the stench awful, and disease spread swiftly. Some Jews whose minds had snapped wandered the ghetto vacantly, in search of relatives who had perished. Others froze to death during that winter of 1941-42. That's when I was conceived, in February 1942.

When my mother's pregnancy began to show, she sought to keep out of sight of the SS lest they murder her, as they had other pregnant Jewish women. As it was, she had close calls. On one occasion, for example, the SS rounded up Jews, including my mother

29

and father, on *Plac Zgody* ("Peace Square"), the largest open space in the ghetto, to send them to the death camps. Such "selections," too, had become familiar events. In March 1942, the SS had marched 50 Jewish intellectuals from *Plac Zgody* to cattle cars bound for Auschwitz. In early June they had packed off 7,000 for Belzec. In October there was a selection of about 6,000 more for another train to Belzec, and in the process the SS had shot about 600 additional Jews for good measure.

During the new selection, my mother recalled, "Everybody was saying, 'Eda will go [to the death camp] because she is pregnant—they will take her right away,' and everyone was crying." However, amid the chaos, she said, "Somebody came—I still don't know who it was—and they took us out from there. When I came back to the room where I lived, only I was left, alone with my husband." The other families had been sent to their deaths.

Years later I also was told that my mother once tried to end her pregnancy (I never learned what she had done or whether my father had known about it or approved), but her attempt obviously failed, and I entered this world about a month after the close call at *Plac Zgody*. When my mother went into labor, on November 18, 1942, a woman gynecologist friend arranged for a secret, late-night visit to the Krakow Ghetto hospital where, my mother told me, I was born under crude conditions—in a cold room, the window covered with a sheet, a single candle for light. Afterward my mother was sick, but "they immediately took me out of the hospital and back to the apartment," she said, slipping past the Gestapo with the newborn—me—in a shopping bag carried by the gynecologist.

There was always gossip in the ghetto about more "selections" on the way, and with each new rumor my parents grew more desperate, as reflected in the letter my mother finally sent to Zofia Sendler. "I beg you," she wrote, "you are a mother as well, save my child… Give her food and keep her clean… be her mother and give her love, because I her unhappy mother cannot give her anything…"

Chapter 1. In the Shadow of the Shoah

My mother reminded the Sendlers that my family had some means and, assuming this would remain the case after the war, said that whatever happened they would be rewarded in this world as well as in the next. Accompanying the letter was a document showing that if my parents did not survive, they wanted me to inherit the family's estate. In addition, my father sent a separate note promising the Sendlers money after the war or, if they preferred, his one-fifth share in the family home.

Through a family friend, my father was the one who had made the arrangements for the Sendlers to hide me. I was told about that years later when I asked how my mother could have given me away, especially after she had dodged the SS and come so close to being killed before bringing me into the world. I could not fathom how she could then give me to strangers. While some other Jewish parents in Krakow also hid their young—in Catholic homes, convents, monasteries, orphanages, boarding schools and elsewhere—the overwhelming majority found it impossible to let go of their children. It is not hard to understand why they held on to them, taking them to the ghettos, the labor camps, even the concentration camps. That, however, is why the children ended up as little bodies in ditches or ashes in ovens. My father believed that unless I was smuggled out, I, too, surely would die, and he convinced my mother of this. So the arrangements were made.

There were several ways to smuggle people, food, letters, valuables and other items in or out of the Krakow ghetto. Some did it through a pharmacy called *Under the Eagle*. The pharmacy, overlooking *Plac Zgody*, was one of the few non-Jewish establishments that the Germans had allowed to continue operating inside the ghetto walls. The owner, a remarkable man named Tadeusz Pankiewicz, had declined an SS offer to swap his store for a confiscated Jewish pharmacy outside the ghetto, and he was the only non-Jew who actually lived in the ghetto as well. Pankiewicz and his three women assistants gave considerable aid to frantic

Jews. Among other things, during "selections" for the death camps Jews hid in his pharmacy and sometimes escaped through the rear door; he and his staff also provided bandages for those who had been shot, their limp bodies littering the square. Other times Jews smuggled food, letters and valuables in and out of the ghetto through the *Eagle*. In addition, Pankiewicz provided sedatives for hidden Jewish children to prevent them from making noise, hair dye for older adults to make them look younger in order to escape death, a meeting place for the Krakow underground as well as for artists, doctors, lawyers and scholars, and a hiding place for some Torah scrolls.

The pharmacy, though, was not the only smuggling option. Others bribed one of the Polish, German or Jewish policemen who guarded the four ghetto gates. Still others sneaked into one of the groups with permits to work beyond the ghetto walls. Before returning to the ghetto later in the day with the work brigade, the person could remove his Star of David armband and try to secure bread, deliver letters like those of my parents, collect underground news, or search for a former neighbor or friend who might be mad enough to risk everything to hide a Jew.

In my case my father was the one who physically saved me from death. He did it, my mother explained, at the last moment, when the ghetto's liquidation had already begun, in March 1943, while he and my mother were among thousands walking across the city to Plaszów, the Krakow camp memorialized in *Schindler's List*. My parents had put me in a leather satchel after giving me a sedative so that I would not cry and draw the attention of the SS. Although SS men were stationed at intervals to herd the Jews along, my father took the bag and managed to slip away when they rounded a corner. He quickly stopped a taxi (the driver didn't want to take a Jew, at least not until my father gave him his watch), delivered me to the Sendlers, and returned to the ghetto exodus, to be with my mother in Plaszów.

Chapter 1. In the Shadow of the Shoah

My father also left a photograph of my mother with the Sendlers, the one in the museum exhibit. On the back my mother had written, "This is Anita's real mother," so that whatever happened to her, I would at least know what she had looked like.

Chapter 2
Hotter Hells

> People talk sometimes about a "bestial" cruelty, but that is a great injustice and insult to the beasts; a beast can never be so cruel as a man....
> —*Fyodor Dostoyevsky,*
> *"The Brothers Karamazov"*

The Sendlers took precautions to conceal my identity. They obtained a false birth certificate for me under the name "Anya Kasperkevitch." During nice weather they took me out in a stroller on alternate days with their own daughter, Danuta, who was just about my age and had a similar appearance. If anybody noticed that there were two baby girls of similar age in the family of five (Zofia also had two sons), the Sendlers told them I was the daughter of a deceased relative. The Sendlers also had me baptized under my false name, and they placed a little silver cross on a chain around my neck.

None of this, however, stopped a neighbor from reporting Zofia to the Germans. As a result, when the bell at the Sendler home rang one night, Zofia opened the door to find two SS men standing there. They gave her a terrible fright. "You have a Jewish child," one SS man said accusingly. Not true, not true, Zofia protested, trembling, pretending to be horrified at the very idea of harboring "a filthy Jew." The SS asked for her papers and for my birth certificate. She showed them both, as well as the baptismal certificate for Anya Kasperkevitch, and she swore on a Bible that I was not Jewish. To Zofia's immense relief, the SS men left without taking further action.

Chapter 2. Hotter Hells

At the same time, my real parents had begun to suffer in the hotter hells of Hitler's camps. First, in Plaszów, they fell under the harrowing reign of Amon Goeth. Plaszów was principally a labor camp then, and, because of my father's history of working with leather, my parents were assigned to a workshop where prisoners produced shoes. Commandant Goeth, however, was not a man to be content with supervising slave enterprises. The child of a privileged family in Vienna, Goeth grew up to become a sadist who loved to torture and kill people, especially Jews. He relished public hangings, whippings, shooting prisoners in the head, ferocious dogs ripping apart Jews or, as depicted in a famous scene from the film *Schindler's List*, firing his telescopic sniper rifle from his villa balcony to murder prisoners below, as if they were so many cardboard targets.

Inmates had little to eat, little chance to wash, and one hole in a concrete slab that was called a latrine. What were plentiful were *appells*—roll calls. There was an *appell* each morning and an *appell* later in the day, to make sure no one had escaped. The *appells* usually were terrifying experiences. As one of my mother's young friends, Lusia Avnon (née Luszczanowska), has written, "Every count had its own rules. Sometimes every eighth prisoner was executed, at others every third one was given 25 lashes. Why? Because! No reasons were necessary in Plaszów."[*]

Above all, Plaszów confirmed for my parents how right they had been to smuggle me to the Sendlers. Other parents had managed to take several hundred children with them to Plaszów, hiding them in the barracks. That did not please Goeth, who was aware that they were there. He wanted to have the children killed and devised a scheme to do so. To gather them together, he persuaded the parents to put them in a special building called the *Kinderheim*, or children's home. There, he said, the children would receive special treatment, as

---

[*]   Perry, Idit, *Gisha and Lucia Avnon: Life Story* (Tel Aviv, 2007), 70.

the parents could see anytime they wished to visit them. The parents at first couldn't have been happier—until one day, after a *selektion*, stunned mothers saw their children being driven away from the camp on trucks. The parents—including two friends of my mother, sisters named Manya and Fela, who each had a young daughter on the trucks—began screaming and weeping. Over the camp loudspeakers the Nazis played a children's song—*Mother, don't cry when we speak of parting...*—as if to drown out the horrid cries. Many parents ran after the trucks, arms out, trying to reach for their children, to touch them, to say something to them. The SS shot a few of the mothers as they ran. The rest gave up as the trucks left Plaszów. It was no secret where they were going: to Auschwitz, about 40 miles away, where children were quickly sent to the gas chambers.

Until August 1944, my mother and father had to endure Goeth's madness, worrying about who would be shot or beaten next, never knowing if the next moment would be their last. That month, however, my parents were selected for transfers—to still deadlier camps. First, my mother was among thousands of women crammed into rail boxcars that took them the 40 miles to the dreaded Auschwitz. The next day my father, his father and his two remaining brothers were squeezed into other boxcars that traveled several hundred miles—with no bathrooms or water and little air—to Mauthausen, a camp near Hitler's boyhood home of Linz, in Austria. As was common in such boxcars, more than a few Jews did not survive the horrid trip.

Like many SS camps, Mauthausen originally was established for criminals and political prisoners. As Germany conquered more lands, though, the camp swelled with POWs and civilians from Russia, Poland, Yugoslavia, Holland, Italy and Czechoslovakia. It also housed 7,000 Spanish Republican refugees (who had fled to France after Franco's 1939 victory and had refused to return home), plus a handful of captured saboteurs from Britain's Special Operations Executive. The main camp and its many subcamps

Chapter 2. Hotter Hells

had long held relatively few Jews. With the need for slave labor growing as the war progressed, however, the SS shipped thousands of mainly Hungarian and Polish Jews, including my father, to Mauthausen from March to December of 1944. He was prisoner Number 85239.

SS policy toward those Jews was overwhelmingly of the work-them-to-death variety. The principal work was in a granite quarry called the *Wiener Graber*; the city of Vienna (*Wien*) owned the quarry and long had used its stones to pave its streets. Now Hitler wanted granite boulders from the quarry for extravagant buildings that he planned for his childhood home of Linz. These included, among others, a Führermuseum complex that was to display artworks the Nazis had accumulated, including the public and private art they had looted (some of it from Jewish collectors), an elaborate opera house, and an Adolph Hitler Hotel. Therefore, frail, underfed prisoners, including my father and his father and brothers, were forced to transport granite boulders from the quarry in wooden boxes strapped to their backs. Rows of prisoners carried them as quickly as possible up 186 steps, known as "The Stairs of Death," and then on an uphill road for over half a mile more. Although most prisoners were not expected to live very long, SS guards, for their amusement, sometimes hastened their demise. Some guards beat prisoners or butchered them in the quarry. Others ordered them to fight each other on a cliff above the quarry, at a spot known as "The Parachute Jump." After the losers plummeted to their deaths below, the guards pushed the winners off the cliff as well. Not surprisingly, some prisoners committed suicide by jumping off on their own (while others in Mauthausen, as in other camps, chose to throw themselves on the camp's electrified barbed-wire fences). In all, more than 14,000 Jews were murdered in Mauthausen—and for absolutely nothing so far as the granite boulders were concerned. Hitler never erected a single grand building in Linz.

At Auschwitz, where my mother went, on the other hand, the Nazis employed slave labor for serious war work. At least

37

that was so in nearby Auschwitz III-Monowitz and its subcamps, which included, among other facilities, a large I.G. Farben chemical complex to produce synthetic rubber and liquid fuel, a Krupp armaments plant, and a Siemens airplane factory. My mother, however, never saw Auschwitz III. When she and the other women straggled off their train, the SS screamed at them to line up and move toward the entrance to Auschwitz I, the central camp. On the way they encountered Dr. Josef Mengele, flicking his riding crop to indicate who would go to the gas chamber (flick—to the left) and who would live (flick—to the right). A cold and meticulous man born to prosperous parents, Mengele was not the only SS doctor at Auschwitz or other killing camps to perform these life-and-death selections. He was, however, the one most often at the Auschwitz railhead when prisoner trains arrived, because he was searching constantly for fresh supplies of identical twins, dwarfs and others on whom he could perform his grisly medical "experiments."

That summer day in 1944, Mengele spared my mother, flicking his riding whip to the right. My mother was relieved to see, moreover, that he had sent her in-laws and friends from Plaszów to the right as well. They included my father's mother, Sarah, and her other daughter-in-law, Ella, who was married to my father's brother Monyek. Also sent to the right were several of my mother's good friends, including Cyla Markowska, Miriam Luszczanowska and Miriam's daughters, Helga and Lusia. SS guards led all these "lucky" women to a barrack and ordered them to remove their clothes. The guards then shaved off all of their bodily hair and took them to a shower.

"We were standing naked," my mother said, "and I was ashamed. One man who was working there—he knew me from Krakow—came to me and said, 'Maybe you want bread or something,' but I didn't want anything. I was depressed and cold. Other men came to see us. 'Do we know somebody?' they would ask. But I didn't want to talk to them. I was ashamed."

Chapter 2. Hotter Hells

The guards then gave each of the women a striped dress. The next day they were marched to Auschwitz II-Birkenau, the killing camp, which had multiple gas chambers and crematoriums. There SS women with tattooing needles "branded" their arms. My mother became Prisoner A-17651.

There was no work for prisoners in Auschwitz II-Birkenau, though a Polish woman who was assisting the Nazis there did provide a chore for my mother. "She said, 'When you will wash my shirts, I will give you more soup,'" my mother recalled. "So I was washing the shirts, and she was bringing me soup, which I was sharing with my mother-in-law and my sister-in-law." Mostly, though, Auschwitz II was a place for killing, for hunger amid the stench of burning flesh, for more daily roll calls and for punishments, whether for the guards' sadistic pleasure or a prisoner's disobedience or both. A friend of my mother who spoke back to an SS woman, for instance, had to endure a form of waterboarding: She was forced to kneel near the laundry and throw back her head while hot and cold water were poured over her, one after the other, over and over, until she passed out.

Inmates who did not have specialized skills that the Germans needed at Auschwitz III but who were still capable of performing work were soon transported to other camps. My mother was among those chosen to work elsewhere, but she was reluctant to go. "I didn't want to leave my elderly mother-in-law," she explained. "I had promised that I would stay with her." But then my grandmother fell ill and was sent to the Auschwitz hospital, where the staff included Jewish doctors whose help the Nazis needed. Much to my mother's surprise, her gynecologist friend from the Krakow ghetto, the woman who had delivered me, was among them. (I have always wanted to thank her in some way, but I have never known her name or whether she survived.) "You go—go with the transport!" she exhorted my mother. "Don't stay here! They are going to put you all in the gas chamber!"

39

Part I. Origins

With my grandmother still in the Auschwitz hospital (from which nobody ever returned), my mother was shipped in late fall of 1944 to a labor camp, Nieder-Orschel, in Tieringen, Germany. That camp, where she worked on ammunition for planes, was no paradise, but inmates did at least get larger food rations than the cup of black coffee, occasional piece of bread and bowl of soup that the women survived on at Auschwitz. The barracks also were smaller, cleaner and less crowded. Inmates woke later to go to work, killing machines were gone, and beatings were rarer.

At Tieringen, my mother and several others tried to sabotage the factory's efforts, flushing parts they were working on down the toilet. "They didn't catch us ever," my mother said. When the Nazis did uncover sabotage, they became furious, but even then the punishment was mild, involving a relatively brief denial of food. This was because at that point in the war—early 1945—the Nazis sorely needed prisoners to make everything possible for a badly stretched Luftwaffe that was incapable of deterring Allied and Soviet advances into Germany or the bombs raining on the Fatherland, including those that fell near Tieringen and other camps.

It soon became clear to all that the war was near its end. The Tieringen plant closed, and the prisoners were sent to Bergen-Belsen, near Hanover in northwest Germany. By then, Bergen-Belsen had become a collection center for evacuees from a number of other camps, especially those near advancing Allied forces. The early 1945 arrivals included, once more, her sister-in-law Ella, Cyla Markowska, and Miriam Luszczanowska and her daughters. The Bergen-Belsen population swelled far beyond the camp's capacity to provide food, water, shelter or sanitation. As a result, diseases, especially typhus and dysentery, spread more swiftly than usual. Inmates sometimes went for days without anything to eat. "Bergen-Belsen was the worst camp," my mother said. "People didn't even know if they were people... Every day thousands were dying."

40

Chapter 2. Hotter Hells

As the war came still closer, my mother fell victim to typhus herself, developing a high fever, nausea, a persistent cough and a spreading rash. She grew weaker daily. "I'm dying," she told Ella. Her worry, she said, was that nobody would return to Krakow to search for her daughter.

But Ella and others would hear none of it. "You cannot die," Ella replied. Cyla found water for her and nursed her as best she could. I remember my mother telling me that her strangest helper was an SS woman in the Bergen-Belsen kitchen where she had been put to work. Aware that Allied forces were not far from Bergen-Belsen, the SS woman helped my mother stand up and told her to keep coming to the kitchen every day, to pretend to be working, so that no more harm would befall her. In this way she kept my mother away from the infirmary—where an orderly was known to be killing badly stricken inmates—and shielded her from some SS guards and others who were shooting at or beating sick prisoners.

Finally, on April 15, 1945, British soldiers of the 11th Armored Division liberated Bergen-Belsen. They were, naturally, aghast, unable to believe what they saw: about 60,000 emaciated and sick prisoners like my mother and more than 13,000 unburied corpses piled on the ground, with many who were still alive lying and moaning among them. A BBC broadcaster reported: "A mother, driven mad, screamed at a British sentry to give her milk for her child, and thrust the tiny mite into his arms, then ran off, crying terribly. He opened the bundle and found the baby had been dead for days." One liberator recalled fellow soldiers pushing cigarettes and sweets through the barbed wire to Bergen-Belsen inmates. The inmates fell on them so ferociously that some were killed in the scramble.

Initially, the British began excavating mass graves and bull-dozing corpses into them. But they soon decided to make Germans from nearby towns do the job, along with the handful of SS men and women who had not fled. The Germans loaded thousands of diseased corpses onto trucks, or directly into mass graves, for burial. The British in the end would burn the camp to eradicate the diseases, but first they tended to the living. Medical units began treating survivors, moving them through a delousing facility and then to a hospital established in a military barracks next to the camp.

"At first, I didn't believe that the British had freed us," my mother recalled. "But then they gave us a piece of bread. They asked who had typhus, and my friends said me." At that point my mother collapsed and did not regain consciousness for about two weeks. When she came to, she had a high fever and asked where she was. "You are in a hospital—and you are free," a nurse replied. "For a long time I was in the hospital," my mother said. "There were a lot of sick people, a lot," and the British soon needed volunteers among survivors to help care for those who were the sickest. "I was very sick, but they said, 'Who can help?' So I said that I could... I was a nurse... They were dying in my hands." Indeed, despite the medical care, 9,000 liberated inmates died in the first two weeks after the British arrived, and 4,000 more perished in May. Some patients' diseases simply were too advanced to save them. Others tragically devoured more of the food that the British and the Red Cross supplied than their skeletal bodies could process and tolerate.

The British asked my mother one day if they could contact somebody to let them know that she was alive. Part of my mother's memory, however, temporarily failed her. From the awful news that she had received while she was still in the Krakow ghetto, she knew that the Nazis had murdered her parents, Chaim and Rivka Dükler, and her youngest sister, Danusha, in their hometown of Zawoje. Her father had been hiding in the woods, but when he learned that the SS had taken his wife and daughter, he returned, choosing to die with them; they were shot and their bodies dumped with others into a mass grave. She also knew that a second sister, Irena, had been murdered by the SS in Lemberg because she had refused

Chapter 2. Hotter Hells

to wear her armband. A third sister, Tosha, had been killed in the death camp of Treblinka. But my mother had a fourth sister, Lucia, the oldest, who was still alive. She had been married in England shortly before the war. My mother tried to remember her sister's married name and her address in Great Britain, but it just wouldn't come to her.

What she was far more concerned about, at any rate, was the fate of my father. She asked everyone she encountered—doctors, nurses, other survivors, a rabbi, British soldiers—whether they knew what had happened to him. She kept asking until the rabbi with whom she had spoken came to her one day with information from others who had been at Mauthausen: My father, who had worked in the granite quarry and had been beaten by the SS guards, had been murdered there, together with his father and his remaining brothers. That news weighed heavily on my mother, who became quite depressed when she learned of it. My father's death has also long weighed on me: I never had a chance to know him, let alone to hug him and thank him for everything he did to keep me alive. I later learned that he had died just two-and-a-half months before a platoon from the U.S. Third Army liberated Mauthausen in May 1945.

For no reason she could explain, while my mother was helping open Red Cross packages at the hospital one day, she suddenly remembered the married name of her sister in England—Lucy Bernard—as well as her address outside London. She gave the information to the British. "They contacted my sister and my brother-in-law," and my joyous aunt and uncle immediately sent her a package of clothing and packaged foods. The British then offered to send her to her family. They were stunned when my mother told the British and her sister that she could not go. She explained that she had given birth to a baby girl in the Krakow ghetto, that the baby had been hidden with a Catholic family in Poland and that she had to find out what had happened to her. Was she alive? Had she been hurt? Had she been abused? Was she still at

43

the Sendlers' home in Krakow? Had they given her away? She knew that she would have to return to Krakow to get the answers.

She asked friends from Krakow—Helga and Lusia Luszcza-nowska (their mother Miriam had died in Bergen-Belsen two days before the camp was liberated) as well as Ella—whether they wanted to go back with her. Ella declined, as did Helga, but 17-year-old Lusia was eager to return. She reminded her older sister that they had long vowed to go back to wait for whoever had survived, particularly their father, Herman (who was a friend of my father's family from the leather business), even though several Mauthausen survivors at Bergen-Belsen had told her that her father, too, had been worked to death in the granite quarry.

My mother and Lusia began preparing for their trip in early June. They had modest funds, provided by Jewish relief agencies such as the American Jewish Joint Distribution Committee (known as "The Joint") and the United Nations Relief and Rehabilitation Administration (UNRRA). My mother was still weak from her illness, and Lusia's body remained bloated. When a British doctor examined Lusia to certify that she could take the trip, he told his nurse, in English: "This girl can't go to Poland. She won't live more than two or three weeks anyway. She's filled with fluid." To his surprise, Lusia—who originally had thought it absurd for her mother to arrange for her to learn English in the Krakow ghetto from a British woman who had married a Polish Jew—replied, "Don't worry. Just give me the certificate, and I'll take care of staying alive." Moved, the doctor gave her not only the certificate but also a letter stating, "To Whom It May Concern: Please extend every possible assistance to this young woman. She deserves it," and identified himself as "The Bergen-Belsen Doctor."

"Everywhere we went we showed the letter and immediately received food," Lusia recalled.

Even so, the trip was daunting. Immense waves of humanity flowed every which way after the war. Millions of "displaced persons,"

Chapter 2. Hotter Hells

or DPs, were on the move, in or out of many nations. Masses of POWs were being transported by the Allies to each other from camps they had liberated, as required by the post-war planning accords reached by the Big Three—the United States, the United Kingdom and the Soviet Union—in February 1945 at Yalta, in the Crimea. And, amid the sheer chaos that reigned immediately after the war, thousands of Nazi war criminals were escaping along "ratlines" to Spain or Italy or France or other nations in Europe and then mainly to South America, including via the route of the ODESSA—*Organisation der ehemaligen SS-Angehörigen*, or "Organization of Former SS-Members"—popularized in the novel and film *The Odessa File.*

Jews, for their part, were heading in multiple directions. Those who had fled Poland to Russia when Hitler invaded and had ended up in Siberia or elsewhere were now beginning to return westward. Those seeking to go to Palestine in spite of British roadblocks were moving across Eastern Europe to Germany's American zone and on to nations with Mediterranean ports, usually with the help of the *Bricha* (Hebrew for "escape" or "flight"). That was the illegal Jewish immigration network created mainly by the Jewish Brigade Group, a British army unit of Jews from Palestine. A number of concentration camp survivors, who made up only a small part of the DP population at the time (perhaps 8 percent), traveled back home to the east, at least initially, in search of family, friends and lost homes. My mother and Lucia were among them.

Most of those in the rivers of refugees, one of the largest population movements in history, would end up back in their homelands, sometimes with tragic consequences. This was especially the case with forcibly repatriated Russians, many of whom Stalin ordered killed or sent to the Gulags, and anti-communist Yugoslavs, who were murdered by Marshall Tito. Many of the DPs—from Poland, the western Ukraine, Lithuania, Estonia and Latvia—fought desperately against returning to lands that were under Soviet control. This was not simply because of their hatred for the communists but also because many had fought with the Germans against Stalin after Hitler had attacked the Soviets in mid-1941. Others had joined or were conscripted into the Gestapo or the Waffen-SS and had become, among other things, concentration camp guards. Still others had worked for the Nazis in fields or factories, as volunteers or slave laborers. In all these cases, repatriation would create more candidates for execution or Siberia.

As my mother and Lusia set out, then, an army of uprooted souls crammed Europe's highways—trudging on foot with a few meager belongings from bombed-out cities, pulling or sitting on carts, walking with bicycles that couldn't be ridden because of clogged roads—while military vehicles weaved through the throngs. Train systems, crippled during the war, ran at best in fits and starts, and trains that did run generally were overwhelmed with passengers, many of whom hung out windows or rode atop cars. Nonetheless, my mother and Lusia were determined to await trains that could carry them south to Bavaria, east across Czechoslovakia, and then to Poland and Krakow. The trip, which today can be completed in a matter of hours, took them three weeks.

Their bodies still frail, they had to sit outside rail stations at night and wait for long times, in long lines, for the arrival of another packed train that was moving very slowly—and then hope to get on it. Even getting aboard, however, did not assure them of a ride. Sometimes when they were on board there were sudden shouts of "Everybody out! Everybody out!" The train was needed for troops. At the Czech border they were removed from three different trains, because only those on organized "repatriation" transports, taking refugees back to their homelands, could cross. They finally found a Polish repatriation train, which took them to the Czech capital of Prague, where they had to change trains again.

It was in the Prague railroad station that they accidentally encountered what has become known as the "Greek bluff" in action. They caught sight of two young men from Krakow, whom

Chapter 2. Hotter Hells

Lusia recognized, sitting on a waiting train headed in the opposite direction. They boarded their train quickly to talk to them, eager to ask questions about Krakow, but when they spoke to them in Polish the young men just stared back mutely. When she and my mother rose to leave, Lusia reported, one man whispered that they couldn't appear to understand or speak Polish because they were carrying Greek papers—a gambit of the *Bricha* to help Polish Jews escape to Palestine. The forged documents stated that the men had been in Nazi camps and were returning to Greece. Unable to check this with a Greek consulate, and thinking that the Hebrew the travelers spoke actually was Greek (the *Bricha* drummed it into them never to speak Polish, Russian or Yiddish, only Hebrew), border guards let them cross. As Mark Wyman notes in his book *DPs: Europe's Displaced Persons, 1945-51*, "The ultimate compliment for this ruse came when a group of authentic Greeks was arrested crossing into Czechoslovakia. Their documents were so different from those the guards were accustomed to view that they were charged with having forged papers."

In the Prague station the young men whispered urgently to the two women, telling them not to go back to Poland. They warned that Poles were attacking returning Jews. My mother, however, refused to end her search for her child, and Lusia did not want to return to the barbed-wire fences of Bergen-Belsen. So they looked for another train to take them eastward across the rest of Czechoslovakia. They were lucky enough to encounter some unexpected kindness along the way. On one leg of the journey, a stranger arranged for them to ride with British troops. On another leg, a train of boxcars loaded with Russian soldiers entered their station. Much to Lucia's surprise, my mother started speaking to them in Russian, a language she had picked up during her 19 months in Russian-controlled Lemberg. She told them that she was trying to return to Krakow to find her little daughter and that Lusia was her sister. The Russians lifted them both onto their car to share their ride and even tried to persuade the young women to go back to Russia with them. They of course declined. Soon, weary and hungry and with little money left, they crossed into Poland and stopped at the railroad station in Katowice, where they waited again, this time for the final train to Krakow.

Chapter 3
"Don't Let Her Take Me!"

To part is the lot of all mankind.
—R.M. Ballantyne

In Krakow, the ancient capital of Poland where Copernicus once studied, a city of cultural treasures and architectural distinction, my mother took a streetcar with Lusia late at night to the 10-acre Grand Square, or *Rynek Glowny*. My mother was sobbing and shaking during much of the ride, and Lusia tried to calm her. When they reached the 1,000-year-old square in the city's center, they were surprised to see how the war had spared its Gothic structures, because Krakow had escaped almost all bombing. Then they walked to the house on Jogiellonska Street, a brief distance from the square, where my father had left me in 1943. Her heart pounding, my mother took a deep breath. She paused, just standing there, doing nothing. Finally, she mustered the courage to ring the doorbell.

A middle-aged woman, who was leaning out of a second-floor window, asked who was there.

"I'm looking for Anitka—the child," my mother said shakily.

"You are Anya's mother?" the woman asked, her voice excited. She was using my false name, the one on my forged birth certificate and baptismal papers. "She's not here now," the woman said.

My mother's heart pounded faster. "Is she alive?"

49

Part I. Origins

"Yes, she's alive, she's alive" the woman said. "But she's not here anymore. She's in Katowice" (the city where my mother and Lusia had caught their final packed train to Krakow). My mother burst into tears, and Lusia and the Polish woman began to cry as well.

Between sobs my mother asked, "Do you know… where… they are… in Katowice?" The woman said that she did, that she had an address and phone number, and she quickly came downstairs. She asked my mother and Lusia into the house to talk and have some food. At the kitchen table, the woman explained that it was known in the neighborhood that "Anya" was Jewish and that the fearful Sendlers—who worried not about the Nazis now but about Polish nationalist violence against Jews, part of the historic strain of anti-Semitism in Polish society—felt it essential to move. When my mother asked the woman why she had been at the window so late at night, she explained that the Germans had taken her own daughter to another country as a slave laborer and that she stood at the window nightly to watch for her possible return. Then, after providing the Sendlers' address and phone number in Katowice, the woman asked if my mother and Lusia wanted to take baths, gave them towels, and insisted that they sleep overnight in her daughter's bedroom. They were not accustomed to such kindness.

Filled with excitement and anticipation, my mother slept fitfully. When she awoke in the morning she wanted to return immediately to Katowice, but that was not possible: She was out of money. So she and Lusia left, and they decided to seek help from the Jewish Committee on Dluga Street in Krakow. Like similar committees in other cities, the Krakow committee provided shelter, food and other necessities to returning Jews who were in need and, importantly, posted lists of survivors, updating them regularly as more people and news arrived. People would come daily to see if a relative or friend was still alive. As if in answer to a prayer, at the committee

50

Chapter 3. "Don't Let Her Take Me!"

my mother ran into an uncle who had been in hiding with his wife during the war. "He heard me mention my name, and he turned and saw me," she recalled. The two embraced, and he took her excitedly to his house to see her aunt. After a bite to eat, they discussed what had happened to my father and others they knew. Then, my mother said, "My aunt gave me money to go look for Anita."

As for Lucia, while checking the survivor lists at the Jewish Committee she, too, ran into someone she knew, a friend of her father's, and he gave her some money as well. She and my mother spent some of their newfound *zlotys* on a doll for me. On the survivor lists Lusia also had found one of her cousins, who was nervously awaiting the return of a sister, as well as the sisters Manya and Fela, the friends whom she and my mother had not seen since Auschwitz. Lusia wanted to stay in Krakow to see her old street and the Polish neighbors who had helped her family. While my mother traveled back to Katowice, Lusia went to see Manya and Fela and then stayed with her cousin.

My mother's 40-mile ride on another packed train seemed like one of the longest of her life. She was alternately happy and worried, calm and jittery. What would her daughter look like? She no doubt was beautiful, and she imagined picking her up and hugging her. But what should she say to the little girl? Would she know her? How could she? How would she react?

At the station she found a cab to take her to the address given by the neighbor in Krakow. She told the driver to let her out before they reached the house, and she walked up the street. Outside the home she saw a group of children playing, and my mother's heart started pounding again. Although there were a number of children, my mother walked straight to me, a dark-haired, dark-eyed, malnourished little girl who was eating a piece of bread and salami while talking with her playmates. She came up to me and stood there, bending over a little.

"I'm your mother," she said in a soft, trembling voice.

51

I dismissed her with a wave of my hand. "No, you're not my mother," I said, and turned back to the other children. "My mother is inside."

"But I *am* your mother," she said, trying to hug me.

"No, you're not! You're not!" I said, struggling to push her away.

The woman's eyes started to tear. She asked me softly to take her into my house, which I did. "*That's* my mother," I told her, pointing to Zofia Sendler.

Zofia—who years later recounted details of those days for me—was taken aback when she saw my mother. The war in Europe had been over for several months and, since my mother had not returned sooner, Zofia had assumed that she had died. Indeed, Zofia had already begun to make quiet inquiries about possibly placing me with another Jewish couple, survivors whose own children had been killed. Now my mother suddenly was standing before her. The two—they had never met in person before—went into another room to speak, out of earshot of the children. They seemed to be there forever. When they returned, Zofia told me that, yes, this woman was my real mother. She took out the photo my father had left with her, the one with the writing on the back. I didn't want to look at it. "I know it's hard to understand," Zofia said to me, trying to show me the photo again. I pushed it away.

"Please look at it, Anya."

"No."

"But you will *have* to go with her," Zofia said.

"But I don't want to go! I don't want to leave!" I started screaming, terrible, piercing screams, "Please, momma, don't let her take me!" I cried as I clutched Zofia. "Don't let her take me! I didn't do anything wrong! I've been good!"

I am told that I kept screaming for much of the evening, until I was exhausted and fell asleep.

The next day was one of total confusion for me. My first life, as a little Catholic girl, was ending. I was a frightened three-year-old,

Chapter 3. "Don't Let Her Take Me!"

leaving the only place I knew, the only family I knew, no longer
having the "sister" and "brothers" I knew. Indeed, Zofia's real
children were fearful now that they might be taken away as well,
and Zofia had to reassure them that this would not be the case.

Not that my brief life in hiding had been all sugar and sunshine.
Food often had been scarce in wartime Krakow, and growling
stomachs were not uncommon. I did not know it at the time, but
because of my poor diet I already had developed rickets. Moreover,
Zofia's husband, a shoemaker, was an alcoholic who periodically
was violent, pistol-whipping her and the children and once threat-
ening to throw me out a window. But the Sendlers' world was
the only world I knew. Now I was leaving for the unknown with
a strange woman who told me that I had a name I didn't know,
a family I didn't know, and a religion I didn't know. Difficult to
cheer up, I sat mute, clinging to a doll that the woman had given me.

My mother persuaded Zofia to leave her children with
a neighbor and to take the train to Krakow with us, in part to see
if my mother could fulfill my family's financial promises to the
Sendlers. Zofia's departure did not reassure her nervous children,
but I was not unhappy that she came with us. On the ride back
my mother thought a lot about how finding me had not resulted in
the experience she had imagined for nearly three years, the reunion
she had thought about constantly to keep her hopes alive during
the horrors of Plaszów and Auschwitz and Bergen-Belsen. When we
returned to Krakow, she was too embarrassed to tell Lusia, her aunt
and uncle, or others how I had behaved. Instead, she told them that
the moment I saw her I had known instinctively that she was my
mother, that I had held out my arms and rushed to her, and they
evidently believed that story.

What happened next made even less sense to me than everything
else: my mother's little group of friends in Krakow started calling
me a "miracle child." I did not think that I had done anything to earn
the appellation or the sudden attention showered on me. Moreover,

53

as I learned later in life, others among the approximately 10 percent of Jewish children who had survived in Europe had endured far worse experiences. There was the 2½-year-old who was smuggled into Buchenwald by his father in a sack and who, against all odds, survived that camp, a real-life version of the film fable "Life is Beautiful." There was the 5-year-old who was adopted as the "mascot" of a Nazi-led Latvian police brigade that never learned that he was Jewish. There were the children who survived with their parents in slimy, foul, rat-infested sewers, almost drowning as water kept pouring in on days with heavy rains.

I confess, though, that I enjoyed being treated as a miracle child, and it must have helped to ease my trauma, because I apparently did not get upset when Zofia left with my mother a few days later to go to my mother's hometown of Zawoje in the Carpathian Mountains. My mother had tried first to see if she could retrieve part of the imposing Künstler home in Krakow to keep the family's promise to Zofia, but the building, now under Soviet control, had been divided into apartments that were all occupied, and Jews risked their lives if they tried to reclaim confiscated property. So she traveled with Zofia to Zawoje to check on the more modest Dükler house there. But that property, too, was occupied and under Soviet control and impossible to repossess. In the end, my mother had to settle for giving Zofia some money before Zofia returned in a few days to Katowice. The money had come from my aunt in England. My mother gave most of it to Zofia.

I would not see Zofia and her family again for 40 years, when my mother and I visited Poland in 1985. I asked her then why she had risked her life and the lives of her family to hide me. She said that her mother, a deeply religious woman, had told her that the Almighty had sent a baby girl to her and that she had no choice but to protect her, and so she did.

I have never doubted, of course, that the promised payments made an important difference, especially in light of severe wartime

Chapter 3. "Don't Let Her Take Me!"

shortages under the Nazis. I have often asked myself, however, whether I would risk the deaths of my children the way she did, and I invariably have concluded that I would not. As my mother said more than once, "Zofia was a brave woman." While my mother was unable at war's end to give her the property or the amount of money that she had been promised, my mother and I both sent funds, clothing and food to Zofia and her family on a regular basis for 45 years, and I still send money periodically to her daughter, Danuta, the only surviving member of the family, who stayed with me and my family in Washington for a year in 1986-'87 and whom I last visited in Krakow—with my daughters and older granddaughter—in 2016.

The photo my mother entrusted to Zofia Sendler when I was hidden. On the back it says, "This is Anita's real mother".

My mother and father shortly before Hitler invaded Poland to start World War II.

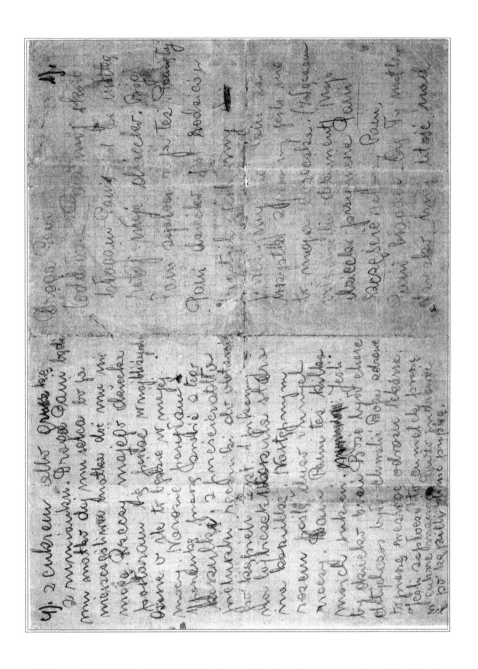

My mother's letter to Zofia Sender, urging her to save me from the Nazis.

Sitting on Zofia's lap, wearing a baptismal gown and a cross.

Zofia (center) with my mother and me at a Krakow restaurant during our 1985 trip back to Poland.

Dining with Danuta, Zofia's daughter and the only remaining member of the family that hid me, in another Krakow restaurant during out trip back in 2016.

With daughters Stephanie (center) and Pam during our 2016 visit to Krakow.

With my husband Noel (left), my brother Harvey and his wife Helene during a 2012 visit to the town in the Carpathian Mountains where my mother was born.

Part II

Closed Doors

Chapter 4

New People, Old Problems

Love, friendship, respect do not unite people as
much as a common hatred for something.
—*Anton Chekhov*

While my mother and I had escaped death during the war, there
was no end to the troubles faced by Jews in Europe afterward.
In Poland, anti-Semitism re-emerged in an array of forms,
including violent ones replete with the ancient fable about
Jews killing Christian children to obtain their blood for ritual
purposes. On June 12, 1945, for example, Jews were attacked in
Rzeszów, about 100 miles east of Krakow, following the murder
of a 9-year-old Christian girl. The girl's mutilated corpse had
been found in the basement of a building whose tenants included
a number of Jews who had been tormented in concentration camps,
in Soviet labor camps and elsewhere, and a "blood libel" rumor that
spread swiftly among Christians triggered anti-Jewish riots. That
pogrom may have been what the young men in the Prague railroad
station had in mind when they warned my mother and Lusia not to
go back to Poland.

Other returning Jews were persecuted as well. Anti-Semitic gangs
murdered many of the *sh'erit hapletah* ("the surviving remnant") in
Poland in the first months after liberation—Yad Vashem puts the
number killed at 1,500 in that period—though assaults on Jews
did not stem solely from anti-Semitism. In some cases, they were

61

rooted in fear that Jews would succeed in reclaiming property taken by neighbors. In others, they were the result of anti-communists battling against the Soviet-dominated regime, which included a number of Jewish officials. Indeed, many Poles viewed all Jews as "agents" of the Soviet Union, an idea that initially had been spread by Nazis propagandists. Whatever the reason, it soon became clear to my mother, Lusia and many other Jews that after surviving Hitler's horrors, they now had to escape Poland's anti-Semites and their Stalinist overlords.

Although it bewildered Jewish communities and others around the world, the majority of survivors sought safety in former Axis nations—mainly Germany, which became a haven for 250,000 to 300,000 dispossessed European Jews, but also Austria and Italy. This should not have been a surprise. Where else were they to go? Arab pressures on the British blocked most Jews from going to Palestine, and just as the United States, Great Britain and others in the West had refused to accept the German Jews whom Hitler had offered before the war, so they were in no hurry to admit Jewish survivors when the war ended. For my mother, Lusia and many others, it was as if the forlorn Yiddish song *Vu Ahin Zul Ikh Geyn* (*Tell Me Where Shall I Go*) had been written for them, and I often think of those outcast years when I hear the melancholy melody and weary words of that composition:

Vu ahin zol ikh geyn,	Tell me where shall I go,
Ver kon entfern mir?	Who can answer my plea?
Vu ahin zol ikh geyn,	Tell me where shall I go,
Az farshlsn z'yede tir	Every door is closed to me

Like most others dispossessed Jews, my mother and Lusia sought the protection of the Western Allies in the occupation zones created in Germany, living in exile there while trying to figure out

Chapter 4. New People, Old Problems

where and when someone might, if not welcome them, at least open a crack in the door.

To get to Germany, my mother and Lusia had to acquire forged papers, needed mainly to get past Russian guards at the Polish-Czech border. They went again to the Krakow Jewish Committee, where acquaintances arranged for the papers. In the end, though, my mother and Lusia, who feared that the Russians would recognize the papers as fakes, decided to get off the train at Bedzin, the last stop in Poland. They left the station with me in tow and walked to a nearby field. My mother then told me to run, and she ran after me. Guards shot at us from a distance, but to no effect, as we made it around the border checkpoint on foot. On the Czech side we were detained for a day, but we then found another train for Germany.

I naturally did not understand it at the time, but that was how my mother prevented me from growing up behind the Iron Curtain and saved me as well from the virulent strain of anti-Semitism that infected many Poles. Indeed, we had gotten away from Krakow shortly before a pogrom erupted there in August. As Jan Gross notes in *Fear: Anti-Semitism in Poland After Auschwitz:* "The August 11 events in Krakow were also incited by a rumor of ritual murder. A Polish mob initially assaulted the synagogue where Jews had allegedly killed a Christian child, and then pursued Jews throughout the neighborhood and in other parts of town."

This is by no means to suggest that Jews had it good elsewhere after the war. On the contrary, in the American Zone in Germany, for example, where U.S. troops initially were in charge, many concentration camp survivors suffered disgraceful treatment. One need only recall the damning words of Earl G. Harrison, the former U.S. Commissioner of Immigration and Naturalization and Dean of the University of Pennsylvania Law School, who headed a presidentially appointed committee that investigated postwar conditions of DPs, particularly Jews, in Germany. In his report to President Harry S Truman in August 1945, Harrison declared

63

Part II. Closed Doors

that "we appear to be treating the Jews as the Nazis treated them except that we do not exterminate them," adding: "They are in concentration camps in large numbers under our military guard instead of SS troops. One is led to wonder whether the German people, seeing this, are not supposing that we are following or at least condoning Nazi policy."

Or one can turn to the notorious diary entries of General George S. Patton, commander of the Third Army and postwar Military Governor of Bavaria, where most DPs were concentrated. One can only cringe over how the physically and emotionally shattered survivors, many looking like the walking dead, were viewed by Patton. In September 1945 he wrote in his diary that "Harrison and his ilk believe that the Displaced Person is a human being, which he is not, and this applies particularly to the Jews who are lower than animals. I remember once at Troina in Sicily, General [Hobart R.] Gay [Patton's Chief of Staff], said that it wasn't a question of the people living with the dirty animals but of the animals living with the dirty people. At that time he had never seen a Displaced Jew."

Patton was the one who directed DP centers to have barbed wire fences and armed guards in watch towers. He defended those policies by writing that if the DPs were not kept under guard "they would… spread over the country like locusts…" He was not happy, therefore, when he read the letter that President Truman had sent to Gen. Dwight D. Eisenhower, the Allied commander, in transmitting the Harrison report to him. "We must intensify our efforts to get these people out of camps and into decent houses until they can be repatriated or evacuated, Truman said. "These houses should be requisitioned from the German civilian population." Patton opposed that idea. As was common in old-line officer ranks, he was far more sympathetic to neat and disciplined Germans than to physically and emotionally crippled concentration camp survivors. He wrote, "I have marvelled (sic) that beings alleged to be made in the form of God can look the way they do or act the way they act." He resigned

Chapter 4. New People, Old Problems

himself, though, to following orders, stating, grudgingly, that "it seems apparent that we will have to do this," though he still worried about mistreating Germans.

A week later, on September 21, he wrote in his diary: "General Louis Craig came in to see me this morning to explain how he had arranged for taking care of the Jews. It has been necessary for him, against his and my instincts, to move 22 rich German families from their houses in order to put the animals in them. I told... him to move the Germans with as much consideration as possible and to give them transportation to move as much of their decent property out as they could."

Then, on October 1, he added: "So far as it is humanly possible, it is my purpose... to see that the density of population per house among the DP's and the German inhabitants is comparable. The result of this policy will be that should the German people ever rise from the state of utter degradation to which they have now been reduced, there will be the greatest pogrom of the Jews in the history of the world." That's correct: He viewed *Germans* as the people reduced to a state of "utter degradation" and almost hoped they would kill many more Jews. It seemed to have escaped him that Germany—with the help of a variety of Western Ukrainians, Poles, Latvians and others—had already perpetrated "the greatest pogrom of the Jews in the history of the world." While a good number of U.S. soldiers certainly treated survivors more humanely, Patton, who was relieved of his Third Army and Bavarian posts in October, was not alone in his anti-Semitism, which had long infected a number of higher-ranking U.S. Army officers.

This, however, was not the sole problem faced by former concentration camp inmates in the U.S. Zone. Because survivors generally were in no shape to perform work, U.S. officials employed German civilians to assist the military. As a result, some survivors ended up under the thumb of their former tormentors. As Leonard Dinnerstein notes in *America and the Survivors of the Holocaust*:

Hence, in one place a former professor, in charge of distributing clothing to DPs even though everyone but the American military knew that he had been a Nazi, refused to give clothes to the DPs on the ground that returning German POWs would need them. In another DP center, in Rentzschmule, an ex-Nazi supervised the activities of former Jewish concentration camp victims. He paid no attention to their needs...

The survivors also had to live among the many Baltic, Western Ukrainian and Polish DPs who had been SS or Gestapo henchmen, who had fought beside the German military, or who had worked in Germany and sought German citizenship before the war ended. These were the ones who most resisted repatriation to the Soviet Union for fear of execution or the Gulag. The U.S. Army, however, made sure that they received equal treatment in DP facilities with Jewish survivors of the concentration camps and killing centers. Remarkably, the military decided that no religious distinctions should be made in the treatment of DPs, that all should be identified solely by nationality and treated equally no matter how much they had suffered—a notion carried to absurd lengths when some Jewish survivors from Germany were classified as "Germans" and treated as "enemies."

Living among their former persecutors caused considerable apprehension and agitation among Holocaust survivors, to say nothing of the discrimination they continued to encounter. The Harrison report assailed this situation as well and resulted in the establishment of separate DP centers for most Jewish survivors.

This was the state of affairs when my mother and Lusia crossed the Czech border into Germany in the fall of 1945 with me in tow. We left the train and went to a little town called Rehau. My mother and Lusia originally had been in Rehau briefly during their three-week journey to Krakow, discovering there a small community of Jewish survivors, including a friend of theirs named Alinka Inslicht. Alinka had been with them in the Krakow ghetto, in Plaszów, in Auschwitz

Chapter 4. New People, Old Problems

and in Bergen-Belsen. She was living now with her boyfriend, Idek Weiden, who would soon be her husband. Idek, who had become the leader of the 50 or so Jewish survivors who had found their way to Rehau, had ties to U.S. military authorities headquartered about 10 miles to the north, in Hof. He told my mother and Lusia that all available DP housing in Rehau had been taken but that he might be able to arrange for us to have homes confiscated from the Germans in Selb, a town nine miles to the south. He contacted the Americans, and the arrangements were made: We would live in Selb, in Bavaria, birthplace of the Nazi party.

Chapter 5
Living With the Enemy

> Anyway, it was one of Maman's ideas... that after a while you could get used to anything.
> — *Albert Camus*

More than one observer has noted how easily people grow accustomed to terrible times. In the United States a friend of mine used to quote his father as saying that the worst thing about the Great Depression was "how quickly everyone got used it." Similarly, E.B. White once remarked, "The terror of the atom age is not the violence of the new power but the speed of man's adjustment to it, the speed of his acceptance." So it was for many Shoah survivors. Even in the ghettos and the camps, many became used to death and torture, skeletal prisoners and gnawing hunger, exhausting work, freezing temperatures, disease and filth—and after the war they became accustomed to living with their enemies, as we did in Selb.

As with many German communities, Selb combined the fetching and the foul. A town of about 17,000 in the northern foothills of the *Fichtelgebirge* ("Spruce Mountains") near the Czech border, it has long been a center of porcelain production, home to such noted firms as Rosenthal and Hutschenreuther. Selb residents, moreover, have created far more than dinnerware or figurines of porcelain. The town has public fountains made of porcelain, a street paved with porcelain tiles, a porcelain carillon that chimes at the Town Hall, and a porcelain coat of arms.

Chapter 5. Living With the Enemy

In 1945, when we arrived, Selb and nearby towns were also home to Nazis and Nazi sympathizers and were surrounded by remnants of Hitler's barbarity. An online travel site, for example, lists one of Selb's "Top 10 Attractions" today as the remains and museum of the Flossenbürg concentration camp, a major slave-labor facility about 40 miles to the south by car. Flossenbürg and its 85 or so subcamps, some of which also were not far from Selb—25 minutes to the north in Hof, for one example—housed more than 95,000 inmates from 1938 to 1945, including German criminals and political prisoners, POWs from Russia, France, Poland, Czechoslovakia and Holland, and homosexuals as well as Jews. The poorly fed, frequently freezing and often abused prisoners in the Flossenbürg system toiled at a quarry, at an airplane plant, at porcelain companies and at other enterprises. An estimated 30,000 of them, including more than 3,500 Jews, died from exhaustion, starvation, disease, beatings, hangings, shootings and, in the end, a "death march" to flee advancing U.S. troops.

Like many Germans, people in Selb generally insisted that they knew nothing of these or other Nazi atrocities, part of perhaps the most remarkable case of mass amnesia known to humankind. Such claims could never be taken seriously, of course, especially in light of Bavaria's long history of Jew-hatred, its support for Nazis—and its citizens' acknowledgments after the war, at least in anonymous surveys, that gruesome events had indeed occurred. By December 1946, for example, nearly 60 percent of Germans in the American Zone were affirming to U.S. researchers that Germany had tortured and murdered millions. The surveys, moreover, identified nearly 60 percent of Germans in the Zone as "racists, anti-Semites and intense anti-Semites." Little wonder that Rabbi Phillip S. Bernstein, Jewish Adviser to General Lucius D. Clay, then Military Governor of Bavaria, told an audience in Munich, the capital of the state of Bavaria, in May 1947: "Gentlemen, if the United States Army were to withdraw tomorrow, there would be pogroms on the following day."

Part II. Closed Doors

As for Selb itself, what did its people think Nazis intentions were when, in 1934, they forced Philipp Rosenthal out of his porcelain firm and had Jewish Deutsche Bank executives removed from Hutschenreuther's supervisory board? (The Nazis confiscated the Rosenthal company altogether in 1937 as part of their "Aryanization" of German industry.) What did they imagine was in store for other Jews when, on *Kristallnacht*, in November 1938, brownshirts across Germany ransacked Jewish homes, hospitals and schools, smashed thousands of Jewish businesses, arrested 20,000 Jews, sent them to concentration camps, and burned hundreds of synagogues, including the one in nearby Hof, where Selb's tiny Jewish community, or at least the few who were observant, usually worshipped?

While no doubt preoccupied like everyone else with their own daily lives during the war, the people of Selb surely could not have been blind to *everything* happening about them. In 1938, for example, Flossenbürg sent its first corpse to be burned at Selb's crematorium, which Flossenbürg used until the volume of inmate deaths there forced it to build a crematorium of its own. Moreover, one of Selb's native sons, a well-known porcelain glaze specialist named Heinrich Hechtfischer, became director of Flossenbürg's Nová Role subcamp, just across the border in today's Czech Republic (then occupied by Germany). Nová Role mainly supplied women slave laborers, included Jews, for a porcelain factory. Some of those workers died in the camp, others after being shipped back to Ravensbrück or Flossenbürg when they were deemed too weak to work anymore, still others on a 1945 death march to outrun approaching Allied soldiers. After the war Hechtfischer was found guilty of war crimes and executed.

More importantly, what did Selb residents think was happening to the town's tiny Jewish community when its members began disappearing in the late 1930s and early 1940s: the merchant Josef Lewi, who perished in Auschwitz; department store owners Rosa and Willi Rosenthal, who were deported to Riga, Lithuania, and never heard

Chapter 5. Living With the Enemy

from again; their daughter Erna Ziegler, who also died in Auschwitz. Other Jews did spend much of the war in Selb—but the Germans never knew it. The town had a slave-labor camp that provided non-Jewish workers—mostly French POWs and young girls and women seized from the Ukraine and Poland—to help keep some of Selb's porcelain factories running. Unbeknown to the Germans, some of the girls—about seven of them—actually were disguised Jews.

By the time we arrived in Selb in the fall of 1945, the slave-labor camp and its workers, including the hidden Jewish girls, were gone. Now, into this defeated and downcast Bavarian town came three more Jews—my mother, Lucia and me—protected by U.S. soldiers from Hof. In line with President Truman's directive, my mother and I were put up in a villa confiscated from a Nazi family, and Lucia was given a first-floor bedroom, living room and kitchen in another Nazi home. This obviously did not please the Germans, but my mother and Lucia did not worry about that. The defeated Germans, after all, were in no position to do anything about it, fearing punishment from the Americans for any offenses against the DPs. As Lucia put it, "I wasn't afraid of those Nazis. They were afraid of me."

After settling in, Lucia took another arduous train journey to Bergen-Belsen and brought back her sister Helga. Helga, who was not as spunky as Lucia, nonetheless liked to tell a tale about the Nazi wife in the house where they lived. It seems that the wife had a collection of fine china, figurines and crystal. "I was washing a saucer," Helga said, "and I accidentally dropped it and it broke. That Nazi started screaming at me. So Lusia picked up a Rosenthal soup bowl and smashed it on the floor and then held a large crystal bowl over her head. 'If you ever speak to me or my sister like that again, Frau Spiedart,' she said, 'you are going to lose a lot more.' '*Bitte, bitte,*' Frau Spiedart said, 'it was just a saucer.'"

So began our little DP community in Selb, which became a regular stop for the *Bricha*'s underground network as it shepherded

Part II. Closed Doors

other Jewish survivors along the same rail route we had taken out of Eastern Europe. *Bricha* trains arrived about every two weeks. Not surprisingly, a good number of survivors who took this route also were from Krakow, and rather than continue on the arduous and uncertain journey to Palestine, some remained in Selb, hoping that another country would open its doors to them.

The first to come, near the end of 1945 or the beginning of 1946, were the sisters Manya and Fela, together with their husbands, Monyek Hauser and Henek Rolnicki, who had reunited joyously with their wives in Krakow. Monyek had survived, remarkably, in Mauthausen after spending time in Plaszow and Auschwitz, while Henek had fled east to the Soviets. My mother was exceedingly happy for the sisters, especially in light of their terrible suffering when their daughters were murdered in Auschwitz. Their husbands' returns, however, also made my mother feel the loss of my father all the more, and she talked to Monyek periodically about what had happened at Mauthausen. My mother also was happy for the sisters when their younger brother, Romek Kaminski, arrived later in 1946. Nobody had known his fate. He, too, had fled east, with Henek, and for more than a year-and-a-half the two had struggled to stay alive in a Siberian timber camp, enduring bitter weather, endless work, exhaustion and constant hunger. The brother used to tell of shivering outside the camp kitchen while cooks inside ground potatoes. Starchy water would trickle out of a waste pipe, he said, and he would drink it from freezing cupped hands to help keep him alive.

Mainly, though, he, Henek and many other Jews in Soviet hands were saved in the end by Hitler, or at least by the Fuehrer's June 1941 attack on Stalin. When that immense assault swiftly drove the Red Army back hundreds of miles across a broad front, Stalin badly needed help from as many sources as possible—chiefly the United States and Great Britain for material and supplies, and the Polish Government-in-Exile in London for extra manpower. Thus in July

Chapter 5. Living With the Enemy

of that year Stalin signed an amnesty with Polish leaders in London and released about 1.2 million Polish POWs, refugees and exiles, about a third of whom were Jewish—including Henek and Romek.

Thousands of those Jews—including Menachem Begin, the future Prime Minister of Israel—flocked to become part of a new Polish fighting force known as "Anders' Army," after its leader, General Wladyslaw Anders, who had been released from a Moscow prison in June 1941. It was a chance for those Jews to eat better, perhaps get new clothing, leave Russia and kill Germans. What more could one ask for? However, General Anders, like many Polish officers and troops, was no friend of the Jews. In fact, he was distressed by how many Jews had streamed to enlist in his army (he estimated that 60 percent of recruits in his initial units were Jewish), and further acceptance of Jews was severely restricted. Polish officers, moreover, badly mistreated many of the Jewish recruits who remained, often viewing them as cowards unfit for soldiering (words they later would eat when the Jews of Israel won stunning military victories against all odds). Many of those future Israeli fighters had acquired part of their training in Anders' Army, which they, like Corporal Begin, had exited after Anders' force arrived in the Middle East in mid-1942 to fight with the British. Anders' troops traveled from Persia to Iraq and Palestine on the way to joining the Allied invasion of Sicily, and, not surprisingly, a wave of Jewish departures occurred in Palestine. That exodus became known as the "Anders *Aliyah*." (While *aliyah* literally translates as "ascending" or "going up," to Jews it means emigration to the Holy Land.)

Faced with widespread anti-Semitism in the Polish Army, other Jews released by Stalin—including Henek and Manya's and Fela's brother—ended up instead in the Soviet Army, which contained about half a million Jews during World War II. The two men did not, however, remain together. They split up when Romek was sent to Moscow for training as a tank officer, a point of great pride for a young man who had been a traveling jewelry salesman before the

73

war. Within the family he periodically beamed as he spoke about this period, especially about commanding a tank in the summer of 1943 during the ferocious Battle of Kursk, the largest tank clash in history. The stunning Soviet victory in that pivotal action, led by General Konstantin Rokossovsky—one of the Soviet military leaders Romek most admired—resulted in two years of German retreats, from city to city, all the way back to Berlin. I would hear about that tank battle for years—particularly after he and my mother were married in 1949.

At the moment, though, his arrival in Selb was simply cause for celebration, as were the arrivals of others. One day, for example, refugees on a *Bricha* train told Lucia that two of her cousins from Krakow were alive and well but were stuck in a temporary DP camp in Cham, nearly two hours south of Selb. Lucia made her way there and found U.S. troops guarding a crowded tent city that contained about 8,000 refugees. Talking her way in, Lucia spent much of the day going from person to person, tent to tent, until, finally, her younger cousin recognized her and took her to her sister. Joyous, her older cousin urged Lucia to find the U.S. army's Jewish chaplain, a man originally from Krakow who had emigrated to the United States before the war. When they met, the chaplain said that he was the son of a Rabbi Shapiro of Krakow—the very rabbi who had married the older cousin and her husband amid the misery of the ghetto (and who had died there with his wife). When the chaplain heard this, he quickly obtained papers and money for Lucia, her cousins, and the husband, and Lucia took them back to Selb to our little community.

The largest influx of Jews into Selb, as into the entire American Zone, however, came after Stalin's release of Jews in the spring of 1946 and on the heels of Poland's infamous 1946 pogrom in Kielce, about 60 miles north of Krakow. The seeds of that massacre were sown on July 1 by a 9-year-old boy who, without telling his parents, had hitched a ride to see family friends more than 15 miles away

Chapter 5. Living With the Enemy

in a village where he had once lived. The boy returned two days later to his worried family—and, to avoid punishment, told his father that he had been kidnapped and held in the basement of Kielce's Jewish Committee building, which housed local Jewish institutions and up to 180 Holocaust survivors. Actually, the boy had returned home with cherries from a former neighbor's farm in the village he had visited, and the Jewish Committee building had no basement to hold either the boy or other Christian children, one of whom, he said, had helped him escape. Nonetheless, the boy's story was swiftly repeated, gaining more dramatic details as it spread—including, yet again, that Jews had killed a Christian child. Before long, on July 4, police, soldiers and a frenzied crowd of thousands shot, bashed in skulls and otherwise murdered about 40 Holocaust survivors and injured 40 others. This deadliest of postwar pogroms provoked panic among Jewish survivors who were still in Poland, many of whom had only recently returned from Russia, and triggered a mass exodus. Poland, Czechoslovakia and Austria soon were awash with refugees as busy *Bricha* operatives helped an estimated 75,000 to 90,000 Jews flee to the West. Little Selb, of course, could accommodate only a relative handful of those Jews as they crossed the border from Czechoslovakia, which had granted assistance and passage to the survivors.

Little by little, members of our swelling little DP community adjusted to life among the Germans while never ceasing to search for somewhere else to go, for a new home in a new nation. I began speaking German, at least outside our house, and early on, because I was thin and sometimes had trouble walking, my mother took me to a German doctor. He found that I was suffering from both rickets and malnutrition. Consequently, my mother began pushing me in a carriage to help keep pressure off my bones and thereby avert the development of deformities. I also was fed eggs, milk, cheese and butter, among other foods, to help remedy the rickets, as well as various dishes to add calories: Polish-Jewish favorites like *gowamki*

75

(stuffed cabbage) and *nalesnike* (thin crêpe-like pancakes stuffed with cheese, potatoes, fruit or other fillings), German dishes like *Wiener schnitzel* (breaded and deep-fried veal) and *kartoffel kloesse* (German potato dumplings)—and lots of cookies. The fattening-up strategy worked all too well: To my great embarrassment, I ultimately become so pudgy that I needed the help of two people at school to do a somersault.

In part, the strategy worked because we had a steady supply of extra food, especially sweets (and other goods like soap), from the U.S. Army PX, brought to our house weekly by a Jewish soldier from Hof. This was in addition to food that my mother bought with weekly tickets she received to shop at Selb stores and monthly packages that arrived from UNRRA and the "Joint." The Jewish soldier from Hof was said to have been young and good-looking, and Lucia vaguely recalled his last name as "Kantor" and believed that he was from South Carolina. I've been told that he brought the extra food, at least in part, because I was the only Jewish child survivor in our region of Bavaria—still "the miracle child" to Lusia, Helga and others. I think that I have seen photos of the soldier in the archives of Israel's Yad Vashem museum. One picture includes two U.S. infantrymen, both lieutenants, at an event celebrating the creation of Selb's Jewish Committee (of which Monyek Hauser, Manya's husband, became president). I suspect that one of those soldiers—he is also pictured at our camp's inauguration ceremony and, in 1946, at our first Passover Seder—was our benefactor, but I have never been able to confirm that.

I remained the sole Jewish child in Selb for more than a year (until Manya and Fela gave birth again), so available playmates of my age were unavoidably German. I was too young, of course, to appreciate the fact that I was playing with children of ex-Nazis or of those who had embraced or tolerated our tormentors. Sometimes, when I shared my supply of cookies with these children, my mother became angry, and I could not understand why. Over time, though,

Chapter 5. Living With the Enemy

she grew accustomed to my spending a good deal of time with German children, the only friends my age that I would have in Selb.

Memories in general, of course, can be quite unreliable, and those of the very young more so than others, but I still recall some of those children. I especially remember a boy named Peter, who was a few years older than me. As our DP community grew and more people needed housing, my mother and I moved into another home with a German family. We lived on the first floor, the Germans on the second. That was how I met Peter, their son. A blond-haired boy, Peter not only was kind to me but he also had a rabbit and a cat, and he let me play with them. That clearly was the way to a small girl's heart. To this day I sometimes look at one photo of Peter and me with his rabbit and another of me holding his cat.

Peter also made me feel safe. I recall one night when I woke up and my mother was not in the house. Frightened, I walked slowly up the stairs in the dark to Peter's room and whispered his name. He said that I could get into his bed if I was wanted. I instantly accepted. Soon, however, he said that he had to go to the bathroom. I told him that I did not want to stay in the room by myself, so I went with him. When he stood in front of the toilet and I saw what he was doing, I tried to imitate him, but I just got myself all wet. It was not the best introduction to spending a night with a boy.

I also had other friends—I recall a girl with whom I picked flowers in the woods behind our house (I have a photo of us doing so), a group of children who played in a nearby courtyard, another girl who invited me to her home for Christmas Eve—but it would be a mistake to paint a rosy a picture of my time in Selb. There also were darker days, especially when I started school. My teacher, Herr Tzopf, was an unrepentant Nazi or Nazi supporter, still filled with hatreds. In class we had to sit with our hands clenched and remain perfectly still. If I moved the slightest, Herr Tzopf would smack me and scream "*Jude!*" You don't forget that. When I came home I told my mother what had happened, but I don't recall anything changing.

77

Part II. Closed Doors

Herr Zopf also was the boyfriend of a German woman named Maria, whom my mother had hired to help take care of me, especially when my mother was working for the "Joint" to assist other DPs—and there was one incident, while I was in our home with Herr Tzopf and Maria, when I nearly died. The two of them insisted that it was an accident, but I have always wondered how Maria managed to forget—for the first and only time—to turn off the gas she had used to heat a tub for me before she disappeared into another room with Herr Zopf. When my mother came home, I was unconscious in the tub, my head thankfully still above water. Frantic, she rushed me to the hospital, where doctors revived me.

On another occasion, I had a disagreement with a car. A friend of my mother's named Yusek was driving and coming to a stop, but my mother opened the passenger door (which I was sitting against, next to her) too soon, and I fell out. The rear wheel of the slowing car hit me, and I was again hurried to the hospital. Except for a broken nose, though, I didn't suffer serious injuries.

For the most part, however, I was as carefree as most young children, dazzled by butterflies, eager to picnic at a nearby lake in the summer, to play in the snow in the winter, and to cuddle with animals year-round. It was the adults, of course, who shouldered the serious worries, including about what to do with the rest of our lives.

Chapter 6
In Search of Home

> The ache for home lives in all of us. The safe
> place where we can go as we are and not be
> questioned.
>
> — *Maya Angelou*

"Home" is a magical word with multiple meanings. For some it prompts visions of a homeland, as it did for Angelou when she went to Ghana in the 1950s and wrote about her journey in *All God's Children Need Traveling Shoes*. For others, it evokes nostalgic pictures of their youths, of hometowns and neighborhoods and houses where they grew up. For still others, "home" means the people or places they love most regardless of where they are, a sentiment expressed in the well-worn phrase "Home is where the heart is."

To Holocaust survivors stuck in Allied hands in Germany or Austria or Italy after World War II, however, home meant something more urgent: a desperate search for *someplace* where they could rebuild their shattered lives, where they could belong again, as they mistakenly thought they had in the countries to which they now could no longer return. You would have been hard put to find any dispossessed Jews in Selb who felt that they belonged there or anywhere else in Germany, and they regularly discussed where they might go next. Palestine? America? Canada? France? Australia? South Africa? Great Britain? Latin America? *For God's sake, where?*

The overwhelming majority of Jewish DPs, as the Harrison Report noted in August 1945, yearned to go to Palestine. Because of this, President Truman urged Britain, ruler of Palestine under the League of Nations mandate granted after World War I, to let 100,000 Jewish DPs immediately into the Holy Land. The British were not exactly happy about that idea and stalled. Shortly afterward, in response to pressures, the British convened an Anglo-American Committee of Inquiry to examine the Jewish DP issue—and the committee also recommended that Palestine's doors be opened to 100,000 Jewish refugees. London, however, simply ignored that recommendation as well, sticking to its policy of placating the oil-rich Arabs—as it had done in its 1939 White Paper reneging on its support for a Jewish homeland in Palestine—and letting in a mere 1,500 Jews a month.

This, however, did not stop the *Bricha*. Its underground network continued to shepherd many Jewish DPs by train and truck—or, more arduously, by foot over the Alps—to Mediterranean ports and onto crammed old ships headed for the Holy Land. To deal with this rickety armada, the British deployed a formidable air and naval blockade. They captured about 90 percent of the vessels and herded DPs aboard into prison ships that took them to detention centers, most on Cyprus, one in Israel—and two back in Germany. That's where 4,500 dispossessed Jews from the overloaded *Exodus 1947*, which had left from a port near Marseilles, finally were placed after the British rammed and boarded the ship about 20 miles off the coast of Haifa. The crew and passengers resisted the boarding party, resulting in the deaths of three and the wounding of about 30 onboard, and the remaining Holocaust survivors were returned in three British prison ships to France, where they went on a hunger strike and refused to disembark. In the end, the British took the prison ships to Hamburg, forcibly removed the survivors from the vessels, and transported them by truck to two camps near Lubeck.

Chapter 6. In Search of Home

Neither the *Exodus'* widely publicized trials and tribulations nor other woes of the naval blockade deterred additional DPs from setting their sights on Palestine. In Selb, for example, Lucia was determined to make *aliyah*. She did so after traveling to Munich and meeting her future husband, who was in charge, first, of the *Bricha* office there and then of illegal Jewish immigration operations in two DP camps in Austria. I also vaguely remember young men leaving Selb to fight in Israel's 1948 War of Independence. I have a photo of a group bidding farewell to one such young man, who posed behind me, with his hands on my shoulders.

My mother, though, was not among those who sought a new home in Palestine. She was weary, worn out from all she had been through, and she had heard "that Israel was very hard… and I was afraid for the hard life. I was thinking that in America it will be better." America, however, was not exactly eager to have her or me. The United States at the end of the war, after all, was rife with anti-Semitism—in jobs and higher education, in housing and government, at resorts and country clubs—and it was not going to put out a welcome mat for more Jews. On the contrary, while there was wide U.S. support for European Jews to be allowed into Palestine, some in Congress were proposing a further tightening of already restrictive immigration laws in this country.

President Truman, however, would have none of that. "This period of unspeakable human distress is not the time for us to close or to narrow our gates," he declared. So, on December 22, 1945, he issued a directive ordering preferential treatment for DPs in U.S. occupation zones, allocating to them roughly 39,000 existing quotas for Central and Eastern Europe and the Balkans, most of which had not been used at the time.

Initially, the directive resulted in relatively few additional Jewish DPs on U.S. shores. This was partly because there were far fewer East European quotas than were needed, partly because far more quotas were available for Germans than could be quickly

81

Part II. Closed Doors

filled, and partly because requirements for often unavailable birth or marriage certificates, health screenings and other procedures slowed the process. (I, for one, have never had a birth certificate. The Nazis obviously didn't issue them for secret births in Jewish ghettos.)

Nonetheless, the first DP ships to arrive at Ellis Island, in May 1946, mainly carried Jewish survivors, which raised eyebrows in many quarters. Despite Truman's plea, after all, America was still determined "to close or narrow its gates," especially against Jews, as evidenced by a public opinion survey that August when the President announced his intent to seek legislation to bring *additional* DPs into the United States. As Leonard Dinnerstein notes, "In late August pollsters questioned Americans: 'President Truman plans to ask Congress to allow more Jewish and other European refugees to come to the United States to live than are allowed under the law now. Would you approve or disapprove of this idea?'" Seventy-two percent disapproved, a resounding rejection. This partly reflected the widespread belief that most European refugees were Jewish (in reality, about 80 percent of the nearly 1 million DPs in Allied camps were not) and the tendency at the time to equate Jews with Communists. Like the Germans and others, many Americans seemed to have a hard time deciding whether The People of the Book were soulless Bolsheviks or money-grubbing capitalists.

Despite the antipathy toward Jews, however, by June 1947 Jewish survivors had received more than 15,000 immigration visas under the Truman Directive, or about two-thirds of the total issued by then—though Jews accounted for only about 20 percent of DPs in U.S. occupation zones in Europe. This feat, attributable in good measure to U.S. Jewish organizations acting more swiftly than others to help survivors through the complex application process, would seem worth cheering about, but it actually helped trigger a major reaction: Alarmed restrictionists in Congress set out to hinder the entry of the many more Jewish DPs abroad, including

82

Chapter 6. In Search of Home

my mother and me. It was only years later, when I had become a lobbyist in Washington and read post-World War II immigration analyses by Dinnerstein, Haim Genizi, Roger Daniels and others, that I understood the legislative obstacles the restrictionists had erected. They usually did not say, of course, that they wanted to keep out most Jews, but consider some of what they did in the *Displaced Persons Act of 1948*:

- THEY SET ELIGIBILITY RULES THAT PRECLUDED THE MAJORITY OF JEWS. The restrictionists picked the date the Truman Directive was issued—December 22, 1945—and insisted that only those who had been in U.S., British or French DP camps by then qualified for admission to the United States. Most Jews, however, had arrived in the camps afterward, particularly the spring of 1946. The December 1945 date was thus designed to exclude about 85 percent of Jews in the assembly centers. (Under the Truman Directive, U.S. consuls had been using April 21, 1947, when admission to DP camps in Germany had ended.)

- THEY LET *VOLKSDEUTSCHE* QUALIFY FOR U.S. ADMISSION—AND UNDER FAR MORE GENEROUS TERMS. An exception to the cutoff date was made for these German-speaking people with Germanic heritages who lived as minorities in other European lands—people whom Hitler and Himmler had envisioned as part of the greater German Reich. Some *Volksdeutsche* had fought in Waffen SS battalions. Others had been concentration camp guards. In addition, *Volksdeutsche* had provided intelligence to the Nazis in their home countries, had received much stolen Jewish property, and generally had been given special treatment by the Nazis. Despite all this, the *Volksdeutsche* now could be admitted to the United States under the German quota—so long as they had entered Germany by the effective day of the statute, July 1, 1948.

- THEY FAVORED DPS FROM THE BALKANS. Indeed, they originally wanted half the immigration quotas set aside for refugees from Lithuania, Estonia and Latvia, where Orthodox Catholics and Roman Catholics prevailed and where many also had fought

Part II. Closed Doors

for Germany (especially against the Soviets they hated so much) or had worked in German war factories or in labor or concentration camps. The final law trimmed the Balkans portion slightly, to 40 percent.

- THEY GAVE PREFERENCE TO FARM WORKERS. Initially, the restriction-ists—who were upset that most Jews arriving at Ellis Island under the Truman Directive had settled in New York City— also had wanted to spread DPs across the nation and to reserve half the quotas for farm hands. The farm number, however, was cut in the end to 30 percent. (Just 3 percent to 6 percent of Jewish DPs were agricultural workers.)

Needless to say, the legislation outraged U.S. Jewish groups, and President Truman had to hold his nose when it reached his desk. Attacking it as a bill that "discriminates in callous fashion against displaced persons of the Jewish faith," Truman said that he wondered whether it was "better or worse than no bill at all." He reluctantly signed it nonetheless—and I will be forever grateful that he did.

■ ■ ■

While the U.S. immigration battle dragged on, my mother received a letter from her sister Lucy in Great Britain. It contained money and two tickets for the Queen Mary, the luxury liner that had been converted to a troop ship during the war but that returned to passenger service, and its original opulence, in mid-1947. We were going to England. Great Britain, inhospitable to Jewish DPs in normal times, was especially so while Jewish guerillas in Mandate Palestine were killing Britons to make sure they terminated their control of the Holy Land. Indeed, in the summer of 1947 the hanging of two British sergeants—in retaliation for Britain's execution of three Zionist fighters—triggered anti-Jewish riots in Manchester, Liverpool and Glasgow and other violence against Jews in Bristol,

Chapter 6. In Search of Home

London and elsewhere. This was atop continuing Jewish ill will toward Britain because of the mistreatment of Jewish DPs on the *Exodus.* My mother, however, yearned to see her sole surviving family member and to bring her daughter with her, so she was excited about the trip. What she was unhappy about was leaving Romek Kaminski behind in Selb. She had grown deeply attached to him, as had I. He took care of me once, for example, when my mother went to a health spa for treatments. To the astonishment of neighbors, he rolled me through the streets of Selb in my bed from our house to his. I remember laughing all the way.

He and my mother were already thinking of marriage and of trying to go to the United States, in part because of President Truman's calls for better treatment of Jewish DPs. Truman supported Jewish positions both before World War II and after. In May 1939, for example, he had attacked Britain for recanting on its commitment for a Jewish homeland in Palestine. In October 1946, on the eve of the holy day of Yom Kippur, he announced support for a "viable Jewish state in an adequate area of Palestine." A year later he backed the United Nations' Partition Plan for Palestine, and on May 14, 1948, when Ben Gurion proclaimed the birth of a new Jewish state, Truman recognized Israel the same day. Even if Jewish leaders' expectations sometimes exasperated Truman—he once remarked that "Jesus Christ couldn't please them when he was on earth, so how could anyone expect that I would have any luck?"— he clearly was a friend.

Romek's sisters Manya and Fela and their husbands also had their sights set on New York City, where relatives were willing to sponsor all of us. Getting into the United States, however, was problematic, and not only because of the then-stalled immigration legislation and its discrimination against Jewish DPs. There was another complicating factor: Romek's service in the Red Army. Romek understandably was proud of having fought and killed Germans. For the United States, however, Germany was no longer the enemy. The new foe swiftly had become Stalin, who, in a February 1946 speech, caused a stir by predicted a coming clash with capitalism. Two weeks later George F. Kennan, U.S. envoy in Moscow, sent Washington his famous "long telegram," arguing that the Soviets were unalterably opposed to the United States and the West and urging American leaders to contain the Soviet threat. Then, in a widely noted speech in Truman's home state of Missouri, former British Prime Minister Winston Churchill declared that a Soviet "iron curtain" was descending across much of Europe and that Soviet expansionism had to be opposed. An infuriated Stalin equated Churchill to Hitler and termed his remarks "a call to war against the Soviet Union."

Thus began the Cold War. All of this sent Americans searching for communists in every closet—in government offices, in schools, in the entertainment world, in the defense industry and elsewhere. In 1946, for example, the House Un-American Activities Committee (HUAC) investigated alleged communist "front" organizations, carrying on a history of House inquiries into alleged subversive groups and individuals that dated back to 1919, following the Russian Revolution. Then, after brief closed hearings on federal worker loyalty in July 1946, a House Civil Service subcommittee found that Washington needed protection from "individuals whose primary loyalty is to governments other than our own." Under these and other pressures, President Truman in March 1947 issued an executive decree creating the "Federal Employees Loyalty Program," which investigated 3 million workers and fired more than 300 of them. In addition, the Attorney General created an extensive list of "subversive organizations" to help U.S. "loyalty boards" identify alleged federal offenders, and defense contractors, hotels, state and local governments and others adopted the list to deny jobs or discriminate in other ways against more Americans.

Then HUAC pursued what the panel long had deemed a hotbed of communist activity: Hollywood. Of Hollywood denizens hauled before HUAC hearings in October 1947, ten—mainly screenwriters—

Chapter 6. In Search of Home

refused to answer questions about whether they were or had been Communist Party members. As a result, on November 24, the "Hollywood Ten" were cited for contempt of Congress (they ended up spending up to a year in prison). The next day, November 25, marked the initiation of the infamous Hollywood Blacklist, which ultimately expanded to include hundreds of actors, screenwriters, directors and others whose careers were crippled because somebody had linked them to an un-American activity.

These and other investigations of Americans charged with aiding the Soviets—a prelude to Wisconsin Senator Joseph McCarthy's reckless accusations, at the height of the Red Scare, of subversive activity among government, media and military figures—affected views on DP legislation as well. At the end of 1946, for instance, a report issued by Senator William Chapman Revercomb of West Virginia, head of the Senate Subcommittee on Immigration, stated: "Certainly it would be a tragic blunder to bring into our midst those imbued with a communistic line of thought when one of the most important tasks of this government today is to combat and eradicate communism from this country." Needless to say, Jews were high on the list of those suspected of being communists—so a Jewish DP in Germany who had fled to the Soviet Union and served as a tank commander in the Red Army was not a great candidate for a U.S. visa. On the contrary, the DP Act that finally was enacted in 1948 stated:

> No visa shall be issued… to any person who is or has been a member of, or participated in, any movement which is or has been hostile to the United States or the form of government of the United States.

Romek would have to figure out how to deal with all of this, which was one of the things on my mother's mind as she and I boarded our ship in Hamburg for our 1947-48 sojourn in England. On the Queen Mary I instantly became unpopular with the

87

Part II. Closed Doors

fastidious staff, at least in our dining room. I can't explain why a 5-year-old would do it, but I was determined to remove the sterling silver napkin holders from the tables and throw them all over the floor. I had hurled a good number of them before a steward grabbed my hand and told my mother that I could not remain in the dining room. Unfortunately, that is the main thing I remember about our Queen Mary trip. (Many years later other things came back to me when I visited the Queen Mary in the harbor of Long Beach, California, where it is has been berthed since the end of 1967 as a hotel, entertainment venue and maritime museum.)

I was not as unpopular in the home of Aunt Lucy, Uncle Bernard and my four cousins, Alex, Harvey, Rita and Susan, though I did once drop all the eggs I had collected in an apron from their backyard hen house. While I got to know each of my cousins, I spent most of my time with Alex, who had been brain-damaged at birth and lived most of his later life in an institution. I used to feed him and play with him and sing to him, and we became fast friends. (Many years later, when I was in London for the marriage of my cousin Rita's younger daughter, Alex was brought to the celebration. Bent over in his wheelchair, he became very excited when he saw me. I asked if he knew who I was, and he shook his head rapidly, indicated that he did, and managed to sound out my name. It was the best moment of the wedding for me.)

My mother had mixed feelings about our time in England. Although we did not personally experience anti-Semitism in Britain, she was never entirely comfortable there and was frustrated with communicating in yet another language. (I acquired enough English to get by and, when there was a conversation in English that I could understand, I became, as usual, her translator.) More importantly, while my mother was fond of Uncle Bernard, Aunt Lucy somehow didn't seem to appreciate the horrors my mother had endured, at times treating her almost as if she had come to England to provide domestic assistance for our British relatives. My mother understood

Chapter 6. In Search of Home

that the British had been through terrible bombings and rationing and other troubles during the war, but that was no reason for Lucy, for example, to ask my mother to care for her children and her house while she went on vacation with Bernard. Although my mother felt good that we had spent time with family, after eight months she was ready to return to Selb and resume planning for the future in the United States with Romek.

■ ■ ■

Selb was not the same when we returned, mainly because some of our friends had already left—for the United States, Canada, Australia and, above all, Palestine—and others would leave shortly. Jews from DP camps across Germany, of course, went to Palestine, first when Jews of the *Yishuv* were embroiled in the 1947-48 civil war with local Arabs and then after May 1948, when Britain's departure from Palestine was followed by creation of the state of Israel, attacks by neighboring Arab nations, and Israel's War of Independence.

Others, including Manya, Fela and their families, were to leave before us for America, but we would follow them shortly afterward. First, my mother and Romek wanted to get married, which they did in a civil ceremony in Selb. They also needed to make sure that Romek could get around the restrictionists' December 22, 1945 cutoff date for U.S. visa eligibility and hide the fact that he had been in both the Soviet Union and the Red Army. The solution they hit upon: Like his brother-in-law Henek, Romek would claim that he had been in Hitler's camps during the war and had come to Germany in the fall of 1945, around the time my mother had arrived.

Getting away with this was not as difficult as they may initially have feared. As it happened, the three-member Displaced Person Commission named by Truman to carry out the 1948 Act was eager to approve visa applications as swiftly as possible—and with as little scrutiny as possible—to ensure that all 200,000 allotted slots were filled. "Therefore the commissioners decided to ignore the mandates of the law and process whatever cases came along," as Dinnerstein notes. Similarly, the International Refugee Organization, which had taken over UNNRA's responsibility for finding new homes for the refugees, "did not hesitate to aid Jews in evading American immigration laws." For example, it helped prepare documents for the DPs, "especially for people who claimed to have arrived in Germany before December 22, 1945." As a result of these and other helpful steps, DP entry into the United States surged. "Whereas only 40,000 had arrived by June 1949 [nearly a year after the Displaced Persons Commission had begun operations], during the next six months 81,968 more reached this country."

That was our crowd—and a crowd it was. The troop ship on which we came over, the USAT General Harry Taylor, was packed with soldiers coming home and DPs yearning for their new homes. Male and female DPs slept in separate quarters in steerage, on thin, hammock-like mattress bunks stacked three high. My mother and I shared a bunk on the lowest level so that I could get in and out. Everything in steerage was limited—space, air, toilets—but I think that most people were too excited to worry about that. In my case, I was also too seasick, often going out on deck to heave when the weather permitted. Romek took me to the ship's infirmary several times for a shot, but the nausea inevitably returned again. It wasn't helped, moreover, by the soldiers on the upper deck. When we had been in Bremerhaven for a few days before the ship left, American soldiers we met there had been wonderful to us. They had given me lots of chocolate, Coke and Fig Newtons. But on the ship a group of soldiers leaned over the upper-deck railing and shouted down, "DPs—Bbleeeeccchh!"and laughed when some of us did indeed "bbleeeecchh." Other times I would just stand on the deck staring at the seemingly endless ocean, at the wonder of all that water. There was nobody to play with. In fact, I do not remember any other children on the ship.

Chapter 6. In Search of Home

What I do remember is how the entire ship was out on deck and how it erupted with cheers when we spied the Statue of Liberty in New York harbor. What a sight! Even as a 7-year-old, I felt a rush surge through me. We finally would have a home and a future. We finally would be free and safe.

Part III

The New World

Chapter 7

Becoming an American

This country will not be a good place for any of
us to live in unless we make it a good place for
all of us to live in.

— *Theodore Roosevelt*

At Ellis Island we went through long lines for physical examina-
tions and other processing, and afterward Romek's sister Manya
met us and took us in a taxi to Brooklyn's Bedford-Stuyvesant
neighborhood. I recall seeing trash in the streets there and saying,
"So schmutzig (So dirty)." We would live on the top floor of a three-
story brownstone at 268 Pulaski Street with Romek's sister Fela and
her family.

Bed-Stuy teemed with groups from many nations, especially
blacks from the Caribbean, the West Indies and Africa, who made
up about half the neighborhood then, as well as Jews from East
European cities, Italians, the Irish, and Latinos from Puerto Rico
and elsewhere. I would not always be safe here—in fact, I would
be attacked several times—but that was not uppermost in my mind
when we arrived. I simply wanted to be as American as possible.
That meant changing some things, beginning with dressing like
American girls, not with the *strumpfen* (high woolen stockings),
funny hats and two old dresses that I owned. My mother would
wash and iron one dress while I wore the other, and then I'd switch
again. It took a little while for her to begin getting more dresses

Part III. The New World

and other clothing—hand-me-downs from the daughter of her physician, Dr. Epstein, a heart specialist who employed a woman named Tosha, one of my mother's friends. Tosha managed the clothing collections. (Dr. Epstein, bless him, also arranged for me to attend a Jewish camp in the summer.) I received the hand-me-downs for a number of years; my mother brought them home in large cartons that we opened with much anticipation. I felt as if I fit in now, at least in terms of what I wore.

However, I still needed to acquire more English quickly, and I had a special incentive to do that: Because I mainly spoke German, my school, P.S. 25, initially had placed me in a class for what were then called "the retarded"—children who suffered from Down syndrome and other disabilities. I certainly wasn't learning anything there, and while the pupils in the class generally were gentle and kind, other students considered them weird. I therefore cringed with embarrassment every day. English was my ticket out, and I did everything I could to learn the language. I listened carefully to teachers, to neighborhood children, to merchants and especially to the radio. I practiced out loud almost daily and, to my great relief, it all paid off: I was moved out of the class after the first semester.

After that I made special efforts to learn more English and to eliminate German and Polish influences on my pronunciation—sometimes with comic effects. On the radio, for example, I was impressed by a flamboyant actress from Alabama named Tallulah Bankhead, who had a program called "The Big Show." She spoke in a deep, loud, gravelly voice, using a cross between Southern and British diction and addressing everyone as "Da-a-hling." I was determined to imitate her. To my parents' puzzlement, therefore, I pranced about my room enunciating elongated vowels with a baritone twang. When I debuted my new way of speaking at school, I thought that everyone would be impressed. They weren't. On the contrary, they seemed to think I was strange. My teacher, Mr. Maltash, called me to his desk and said, softly and kindly,

94

Chapter 7. Becoming an American

"I'm afraid that young girls don't speak that way here." He asked another student, Dorothy (Dotty) Isaacs, to sit with me in the back of the classroom and help me with my English.

Dotty was usually exceedingly helpful, though she did not always give me full explanations of English phrases. For example, on the street once I asked her, "What are those words on the building over there?" She said, "You only use those words when you are *very* angry with somebody." It so happened that my father said something that evening at dinner that infuriated me, so, remembering Dotty's words, I said, with great confidence, "Fuck you." That did not go over well. Nor did Dotty teach me about baseball. As a result, when some boys asked one day whether I was a Yankee or a Dodger fan, I said "Yankee," because that was what we had called American soldiers and Americans in general, and I wanted to show how much I admired them. Little did I know that the answer would almost get me banned from our Brooklyn neighborhood.

Thanks in part to Dotty, though, I ended up speaking English without a trace of a foreign accent. I did, however, have trouble with American idioms, and I sometimes still do. Once, for example, I met my husband after work at the *Washington Post* to attend a reception there. I was conversing with some of his colleagues when I suddenly blurted out, to much laughter, "Aha, tit for tit!" It seemed like a perfectly logical construction to me, especially since I had no idea what a "tat" was. It turned out, moreover, that I was in good company, since hardly anybody I asked for the definition of a "tat," or where "tit for tat" came from, had any idea, either. (As I have since learned, it evidently is a corruption of the sixteenth-century British term "tip for tap," or, roughly, blow for blow, but I like my version better.)

That was not the only time I mauled an idiom. Once, discussing Congress with my husband, for instance, I carelessly referred to a pending "lame-dick session." That, I need scarcely say, is also the kind of mistake to cause howls. When I asked others, however,

95

how "lame duck" acquired its modern meaning, again, few knew that it began as a financial term (referring to eighteenth-century stockbrokers in London who had defaulted on debts) and wasn't used in America until Civil War days, and even then not with its current connotation of politicians or political bodies containing officials who have not been re-elected.

On yet another occasion, during a meeting at a law firm where I worked, I thought my colleagues were being too hesitant in tackling a particular issue in Congress, so I declared, "You've got to take the bull by the balls!" To which a law firm partner replied, "My, that's harsh." Someone had to explain to me later the reason for grabbing a bull by its horns.

Dotty was, of course, in no way responsible for my idiom idiocies. She was a wonderful instructor. Indeed, as I learned years later during a gracious dinner at her home in a Virginia suburb of Washington, she ended up becoming an English teacher. More importantly, in Brooklyn Dotty became a good friend, one of four I had during elementary school. (I haven't the foggiest idea why anymore, but we called ourselves "The Five Battle-Axes" and created our own song lyrics to the tune of "Glow, Little Glow Worm.") Dotty and I used to watch out for each other, including walking each other halfway home from elementary school. Once, however, my solitary leg of the walk did not end well. When I was heading up the stairs of our brownstone, three boys suddenly attacked me, hitting me, pushing me inside the door, knocking me down and choking me. I didn't know who they were or why they were beating me, but I began kicking and crying uncontrollably, begging them to stop. After a minute of struggling with me, one of the boys said, "Hell, she's no fun. Let's get out of here," and they let me go and left.

Nobody in our brownstone seemed to have heard a thing. Upstairs on the third floor my mother was preoccupied with other matters, and because I evidently hadn't been seriously injured (only

Chapter 7. Becoming an American

scared to death) she decided not to take me to a hospital or call the police. As recent immigrants, my parents disliked getting involved with public authorities, fearing that it might lead to problems. As a result, she also did not take me to a hospital the next winter when another boy hit me in the head with a snowball that had a sizable rock in it, or, in junior high school, when darts were thrown in my back during recess. On that occasion I was taken to the nurse's office at Whitelaw Reed Junior High School, where the darts were removed and the wounds cleaned.

The day I was attacked on our brownstone doorstep, what my mother was preoccupied with on the third floor was caring for my baby brother, Harvey, who had been born a couple of months before, on March 18, 1952. The baby, needless to say, added a new dimension to my life as well as to the lives of my parents. They were overjoyed at having a boy, which I couldn't understand. I definitely would have preferred a sister, someone I could lord it over, someone who wouldn't get preferential treatment, as Harvey did over the years, someone who wouldn't make me feel much less like a "miracle" child. It is not unique to Jewish parents, of course, to give special treatment to sons, to coddle them and shower them with attention; it has been thus with many groups over the centuries. Jewish parents, however, seem to have perfected the art, and my parents were no different. While paying little heed to me, they lavished attention and praise on Harvey and rarely scolded him, even when he deserved it.

Harvey, for example, did some dumb things. Once he stuffed pebbles up his nose. Why? He says that he had seen pebbles in a fish tank and thought that they would help him remain under water like a fish. Did my parents get angry with him? No, they just took him to the doctor, who put pepper under his nose to make him sneeze out the pebbles, and then they comforted Harvey— poor Harvey—all the way home. And that wasn't the dumbest thing he did. One day, when he was three or four years old, he

Part III. The New World

almost jumped out the window of our third-floor apartment. When I found him with one leg already out the window, I quickly grabbed him and pulled him back in. "What do you think you're doing!" I screamed. He said that his breakfast cereal, called Sugar Jets, made him "feel jet-propelled," which is what two children in a Sugar Jets TV commercial proclaimed as they flew away. Great. I told him that he was an idiot. My mother, who had been trying on dresses when I caught Harvey, told me to stop screaming at Harvey, but she didn't say a word to him (of course, she may have been in a state of shock). I do not remember her ever praising me for my positively brilliant rescue.

Okay, I admit that I was not always a terrific older sister. On another occasion, when I was supposed to be watching Harvey in his carriage across the street from our house, I started playing with my friends instead. After a while, I glanced back at the carriage — and I didn't see Harvey inside anymore! My heart started racing as I ran to the carriage. What could have happened to him? Could someone have taken him? Could he have fallen out? My friends helped me search, as did some of the "stone lions" (the women who sat on folding chairs gossiping outside their buildings). Finally, to my immense relief, one of the neighborhood women figured out that Harvey had slipped down into the compartment for diapers, bottles and other paraphernalia that was in the front part of the carriage. She pulled him up and put him back into the main carriage. I told my mother about this when I was back in the apartment, and we had a good laugh about it.

I did not tell her or anybody else, however, about another incident with Harvey: how I accidentally dropped him. I was lifting him out of his highchair one day, and he was wriggling a lot. Suddenly he flipped out of my hands and landed on the floor — on his head. He wailed terribly. I picked him up and rocked him and tried to comfort him. He calmed down after a while, but not me — I was in a panic. Had I damaged him for life? Would he still be

98

Chapter 7. Becoming an American

able to walk and talk as he got older? Would his abilities be limited like my cousin Alex's in England? What had I done? My parents, I was sure, would kill me if they found out what had happened, so I kept this secret to myself and watched Harvey closely for years to see if the head trauma produced any noticeable consequences. Thankfully, it didn't. Harvey turned out to be both smart and shrewd. As a kid, he would take bribes (such as free Italian ices) for giving older boys my phone number. As an adult, he became a lawyer and owner of a prosperous finance company, which made my parents *kvell* (gush with pride). They never felt that way about my work as a Washington lobbyist; that's probably because they never could understand what a lobbyist does. So I came in third in the bragging-rights contest, after Harvey and his wife Helene, a wonderful lady who is a physician (and also a child of Holocaust survivors).

It is remarkable, I think, how well our family did in the end, but it was no easy road to travel. At first my father and mother each labored long hours doing piecework, my father for a shoe factory, my mother for a stocking company. My father often worked double shifts, or 16 hours a day, to earn enough and to save a little for the future, and on top of this he attended night school to learn more English and to study to become an American citizen. (He did, of course, become a naturalized citizen, as did I.) He was a meticulous, if often exhausted, student who kept detailed notebooks. He was also determined, like many other immigrants, to rise in the world. After the shoe factory job he worked as a butcher in a market near our house, on DeKalb Avenue, often carrying heavy carcasses on his exceptionally strong back. I remember how his shoulders and upper back muscles had turned almost as hard as rock, presumably from hauling logs in Stalin's Siberian camp. Above all, however, my father wanted to go into business, and this, too, he did. His opportunity grew out of a loan that he had made to a friend who was buying a boutique hotel, the Iroquois, on West 44th Street in

99

Part III. The New World

Manhattan. My father next invested in a second small hotel that the friend was purchasing and then in others, ending up with minority interests in about seven properties. As a result, he left the butcher shop to manage the first property in which he invested, the Washington Jefferson Hotel on Manhattan's West 51st Street, and he did that for the rest of his life. He, too, had truly become an American.

In my own case, I had important help along the way, and not just from Dotty or Mr. Maltash. At Whitelaw Reid Junior High School, it will be recalled, I had the protection of Henrietta, the head of the Lady Chaplains who worried that I was either an imbecile or insane and who therefore walked me to and from school. I also was exceedingly fortunate to have had a special teacher in junior high. Her name was Mrs. Smith. She was African-American, a fact that I note only because of the immense criticism heaped on many African-American teachers these days. Mrs. Smith was a gem. She used to call me "my Portia," a reference to the beautiful and clever Shakespearian heroine in *The Merchant of Venice* who, among other things, pretends to be a young law clerk and saves the life of the merchant Antonio. Mrs. Smith was worried that when I graduated I was heading for a terrible local high school. So she conspired with the principal at Whitelaw Reid to get me into what was then a much better school, Thomas Jefferson High, even though it was much farther from my home. The pretext they used: Jefferson was one of the few schools in Brooklyn to offer courses in Hebrew. Although Mrs. Smith didn't know it, this was an ironic strategy, because the modern orthodox Hebrew school that I attended in the afternoon did not impart much Hebrew to me. Girls there concentrated chiefly on learning Yiddish, the Germanic- and Slavic-based language of European Jews (and, indeed, of Jews everywhere), in part so that they could bargain with Jewish shopkeepers. Boys learned the biblical language of Hebrew, mainly to prepare for their Bar Mitzvahs. (There were no Bat Mitzvahs for girls in our community

100

Chapter 7. Becoming an American

in those days.) Ironic or not, though, the strategy worked, and I went to Jefferson, where I finally learned more Hebrew.

I did well there academically, getting into all-honors classes, writing for the school newspaper and being named "Miss Jefferson." Thanks to Mrs. Smith, my high school years were some of the best of my life. It was in those years, too, that I thought I might become a Hollywood celebrity, certainly one of the most American of fancies for a teenage girl.

It was near the end of 1957, when I was 15, that my mother heard about a worldwide talent search for someone to star as Anne Frank in the motion picture version of the play *The Diary of Anne Frank*. The news struck a chord with her. She had known the Frank family from the concentration camps. Edith Frank and her daughters, Anne and Margot, had been at Auschwitz while my mother was there; the daughters survived that killing place, but the mother died there after her girls were transferred to Bergen-Belsen. My mother also was at Bergen-Belsen when Anne and Margot were in that hellhole. Both sisters, who had shriveled almost to skeletons, died of typhus at Bergen-Belsen several weeks before the British liberated the camp. Their remains were thrown into in a mass grave.

I do not mean to suggest that my mother was close to the Franks. She was not. But she had known them and their fates, and when she heard of the talent hunt for the Anne Frank movie, she began thinking. She said that I looked in many ways like Anne Frank, that I, too, had been in hiding during the Holocaust, that I was about her age when she died, and that I had been in a few school dramas as well. She thought (what Jewish mother wouldn't?) that I would be perfect for the part. I told her that she must have been joking. She was not.

So instead of going to high school one winter day I took the subway to Manhattan with my mother, to the building where the auditions were held. There we met an assistant to George Stevens, the Academy Award-winning director who was in charge of

101

Part III. The New World

the 20th Century Fox production. The assistant was quite interested when my mother told him that she had survived four of Hitler's camps, that she had known the Frank family, and that I had been in hiding during the war. He asked me to put my hair down and to read for a screen test. I was, of course, terribly nervous and could feel myself shaking, but I forced my way through the audition. When I finished reading, the man, instead of saying thanks-but-no-thanks, as I had expected, asked us if we could come back another day. Was he kidding? Of course we could.

When we returned again, George Stevens was there himself to meet us. Stevens had strong feelings about the Holocaust. As a lieutenant colonel during World War II, he had headed an Army Signal Corps unit of photographers and writers that had been ordered to film, among many other things, the monstrous depravities at Dachau and other concentration camps, footage that was included among the evidence against Nazi war criminals at the Nuremberg trials. The experience haunted him, as it did others who had seen the piles of corpses at the camps, and he did not like to think or speak about it. Indeed, he and other Americans, including American Jews, tended to avoid the subject of the death camps altogether during the late 1940s and the 1950s. That prosperous post-war period was a time when Jews were blending in more, when U.S. anti-Semitism was in decline, when some Jewish groups were striving to duck McCarthyism (in one year, 1952, more than half the witnesses before Republican Senator Joseph McCarthy's committee investigating communist influence in the United States were Jewish). Thus while Stevens felt a special attraction to the Anne Frank film, he did not want to deal with it mainly as a story of the Holocaust. As his biographer Marilyn Ann Moss observes, "Now, confronting the [Dachau] experience again, 13 years later, he averted his eyes from the horror of the camps as much as he could — and as much as the 1950s would impel him to do. No one was ready yet to talk about the Holocaust."

Chapter 7. Becoming an American

When we arrived at his office, Stevens asked my mother about what she had been through during the war and what had happened to me, and he seemed intrigued with the answers. He ordered a photographer to take still photos of me and asked me to do a second reading. When I finished, he and I talked about my history and my school life in the United States. Then he thanked my mother and me for coming and said that he would be in touch.

I had no idea, of course, who else was auditioning for the role, how many others there were, or what was happening behind the scenes. I certainly did not know, for example, that Stevens initially had sought Audrey Hepburn for the part and that the Stevens-Hepburn discussions had come to naught. That was when 20th Century Fox decided to announce its worldwide search for an unknown girl to play the title role, a search that turned into a public relations boon for the film. The announcement triggered piles of letters from girls in the United States and Europe, plus the phone call from my mother that got us our appointment.

Now my mother and I waited nervously to hear from 20th Century Fox. Before long, a manila envelope arrived. Inside was a note from Stevens. He wrote that while I had made a very favorable impression, I had not been chosen, largely because of my lack of professional acting experience. He included an 8 x 10 glossy copy of one of the photos taken of me and thanked me for auditioning for the role.

I have long scratched my head about Stevens' explanation. The person he picked for the role, after all, was Millie Perkins, a 19-year-old model from New Jersey who was also bereft of acting experience. Thus, that could not have been the basis for his decision. It had to be something else. There are, I think, essentially two possibilities:

1. My screen test and readings were really rotten and he was too kind to say so. That's surely possible, and I would have leaned toward this explanation myself if I had not been called back for a second reading.

103

2. More plausibly, I did not have the all-American appearance of the non-Jewish Millie Perkins, and my own Holocaust story probably would have become part of the publicity surrounding the film. That could have defeated what Stevens was after.

Stevens, you see, envisioned a "romantic" movie presenting "Anne as a typical teenager rather than a young Jew slated to die in the death camps," as his biographer remarks. In notes that he jotted in his paperback edition of *Anne Frank: The Diary of a Young Girl*, Stevens "looked for an Anne Frank who was neither tragic nor particularly Jewish—a view that coincided with Otto Frank's preferred conception of his daughter and that depicted the 'ordinariness' of her character in the Pulitzer Prize-winning stage play on which the film was based. Anne must be 'universal.'" I suspect, then, that I was penalized, at least in part, for being a Holocaust survivor, for perhaps looking too Jewish, for not appearing "universal" or American enough.

In any case, I confess that when the film came out I was pleased with the *New York Times* review. It praised the entire cast—except for Millie Perkins. The reviewer regretted as "deeply unfortunate that Millie Perkins… does not rise to [Joseph Schildkraut's] level of spiritual splendor" in his role of Anne's father. It called Perkins "reedy." I hope that it does not seem too mean spirited of me to note this.

Chapter 8
Falling for a Litvak

> A Litvak is so clever that he repents *before* he sins.
>
> —*Sholem Aleichem*

While the Holocaust may not have been the focus of the Anne Frank film, in my life it was always in the room. It was in my mother's periodic screams at night as well as in my own nightmares. It was in family arguments and other conversations, including with Manya's and Fela's families when we visited each other. It was in the air when we met with other Holocaust survivors, who made up the majority of my parents' friends. The survivors often lived in enclaves—in Bed-Stuy, in Crown Heights, where we moved in 1956, in Flushing, Queens, where my parents later purchased an attached home, and in other corners of New York—and they shared in each other's *simchas* and sorrows, from births to burials. Many survivors, for example, were at my wedding at the East Midwood Jewish Center on Brooklyn's Ocean Avenue, and they reveled in the fact that the "miracle child" was marrying and would have children of her own.

The wedding followed more than two years of romance that began on a rainy Friday evening in June of 1961, when I was finishing my freshman year at Brooklyn College. I went with two girlfriends to see a movie at the Avalon Theater on Brooklyn's Kings Highway, but the film (*Return to Peyton Place,* with Jeff Chandler)

105

was not exactly a spellbinder. So I spent much of my time checking out a cute guy in the row in front of us in the theater's balcony. He, too, had come with friends, one of whom evidently knew one of my girlfriends. The two of them chatted on and off during the movie as well as afterward, as we walked down to the lobby.

A crowd huddled in the lobby, reluctant to step out into the heavy rain or squeeze under the theater marquee outside. "Can we give you a ride home?" said one of the boys. "We were just going to stop for coffee first at a restaurant near Brooklyn College. If you'd like to come, we'll be happy to take you home afterwards." My friends and I agreed, so he ran through the downpour to get his car. When he pulled up in front of the theater, we piled in. First, into the back seat, slid the cute guy. I followed him quickly into the back (I was no dummy), and someone pushed in after me, squeezing us tightly together. By the time we reached the restaurant near Brooklyn College, he and I were well acquainted.

His name was Noel Epstein. ("I know—it's like calling an Italian boy Passover D'Arienzo," he said, volunteering a complex explanation of how a Jewish boy got the name Noel). He was in the Army now, a reservist on active duty for half a year. He was home on two weeks' leave after basic training at Fort Dix, off Exit 7 on the New Jersey Turnpike. We spent almost the entire time in the restaurant talking to each other as if nobody else existed. I felt as if I had known him all my life. We spoke about journalism, in which he had majored at NYU, about my college classes, about the Army (I teased him by thanking him for guarding the New Jersey Turnpike for us), and about much else, including my auditions for the part of Anne Frank, my family's Holocaust experience and the languages I spoke. He absorbed everything I had to say and asked thoughtful questions. I suspect, however, that we could have discussed anything and it still would have been magical. There was simply an invisible connection between us. My sole disappointment was that he didn't ask for my phone number (he said later that such

Chapter 8. Falling for a Litvak

questions always made him feel awkward). Instead, as he told me, he memorized my last name and address, repeated them in his head during the car ride home, and, in his family's apartment, hurried to look up my number in the telephone directory. He called in the morning, and we spent the rest of his two weeks' leave together.

There was also another problem: my mother was not convinced that Noel was Jewish. This was not only because of his name but also because he had blue eyes and light brown hair and reminded some people of actors like Ed Harris or Jack Lemmon. It's true that his appearance did not fit Jewish stereotypes, but I assured my mother that he was indeed one of us. Nonetheless, she insisted on calling a friend of mine to double-check, and it was only after Noel came to our apartment and she spoke with him that she finally relented. This, however, did not entirely eliminate her misgivings, because Noel, she discovered, was a "Litvak," the son of Ashkenazi Jews from one part of Eastern Europe (the once large Duchy of Lithuania) who were traditional rivals of "Galitzianas" like us who were from another part (what once was Eastern Europe's Galicia). This could have meant trouble. Litvaks and Galitzianas not only pronounced Yiddish differently and prepared certain foods differently, but they generally were suspicious of each other. Among other things, many Litvaks called Galitzianas horse thieves, while Galitzianas tended to see Litvaks as devious traders, as too clever by half.

While this surely did not create insurmountable obstacles for Noel and me, reference to that old East European Jewish rivalry never really died. It emerged most prominently, in fact, during what undoubtedly was the most embarrassing moment of Noel's life, at a time when we had been dating for many months. When Noel brought me home exceedingly late one Saturday night, my worried mother was waiting up for us and told Noel that it was too dangerous for him to take the subway home in the wee small hours of the morning. She insisted that he sleep on the couch in our living room, giving him a pillow and blanket. Unbeknown to Noel,

107

though, she also had told me to sleep in her bed while she slept in mine, because Harvey (who shared a bedroom with me) was ill, and she wanted to be there if he needed her. So, in total darkness, the amorous Noel slithered off the living room couch, gingerly made his way in the dark toward my room, crawled on the floor to my bed, put his hand at the foot of the mattress, and whispered, "Honey."

Suddenly a shriek filled the room. "Litvak!" my mother exclaimed from the bed.

In a state of total disbelief, Noel fled the bedroom, groping in the dark for doorways, banging his head on walls and door jambs, until he finally reached the couch again, his heart pounding. My father and brother and I slept through it all. In the morning, my mother said little about the incident, and I did not ask Noel how he got the bump on his forehead. The word "Litvak" was thus the worst epithet my parents ever flung at Noel, and their view of him evolved until it actually defied all of their images of Litvaks. In the end, they said that he was too honest a man.

Noel and I became engaged in the fall of 1962 and were married the following year. We set our wedding for November 23, the Saturday before Thanksgiving, because the extra time off from my college classes made it easier to take a full week for a honeymoon. The timing, though, was not propitious: November 23, 1963 turned out to be the day after the assassination of President John F. Kennedy. I remember Noel calling me the day before the wedding, as I was about to leave to have my hair done, and telling me that JFK had been shot. I told him that it was no time for kidding, that I was nervous enough already. He was, of course, not kidding, and the day of the wedding we and our parents discussed whether we should say something about that terrible tragedy amid the dancing and singing and feasting of the celebration that followed. We decided against it, feeling that it would not accomplish anything and might only put a damper on the evening. Rather, all of the

Chapter 8. Falling for a Litvak

guests, when they left, received copies of the Sunday *New York Times* that were piled up at the back of the hall, with its giant headline blaring:

KENNEDY IS KILLED BY SNIPER

AS HE RIDES IN CAR IN DALLAS;

JOHNSON SWORN IN ON PLANE

The next night Noel and I flew to Bermuda. We doubtless paid less attention than the rest of the world did to the historic reports and images that blanketed the news during our honeymoon week, but they were impossible to avoid altogether: the arrest of Lee Harvey Oswald—the former Marine who had spent several years in the Soviet Union—for killing the president and a Dallas policeman; the murder of Harvey himself by Dallas nightclub owner Jack Ruby; the heartbreaking photo of 3-year-old "John-John" Kennedy saluting his slain father's coffin after a requiem mass in Washington; President Lyndon B. Johnson's masterful emergency address to Congress on Thanksgiving Day. It was a tangled tale, and the little Bermuda newspaper we were reading did not prove terribly enlightening. In the end, our honeymoon week was a curious combination of the glorious and the gloomy.

It also was a reminder of how everything can be taken from you in an instant, one of the constant fears rooted in my Holocaust history. I naturally have other traits traceable to Holocaust experiences as well, as Noel has learned well. For one thing, I have long been overly protective of our children and grandchildren. Indeed, I have become notorious for buying our two granddaughters, who live nearby, far too many jackets and coats to make sure that they will never be cold. My older daughter, Stephanie, their mother, has gently kidded me for this, telling me that "nobody needs a coat for every five degrees of difference in the temperature outside," and our pediatrician once chided me—"Shame on you!" he said—for putting so much clothing on Stephanie herself as a baby that she developed a diaper rash in

109

Part III. The New World

the midst of winter. Noel, moreover, has more than once threatened to enroll me in what he calls "Grandparents Anonymous," telling people that I started to shake when I passed stores with clothing that I wanted to buy for the grandchildren.

For another thing, I tend to stock refrigerators and pantries with extra food, a habit I acquired from my mother, who would always keep extra bread and other basics in our house. She regularly threw out old food (in warmer weather the stale bread went to New York's sparrows), and I am embarrassed to say that I still find myself discarding a good deal of extra food that has spoiled. For a third thing, I have at times had difficulty letting myself get too close to people—for fear of losing them. This was particularly the case after a dear neighborhood friend of mine died quite young. That brought the Holocaust back to me with a fury, and it took some time before my worries about death and loss finally faded again.

Beyond this, I cannot stand to view too much violence, whether in films, on TV or in exhibits. This has had some paradoxical effects. I often recoil, for example, from watching Holocaust films, as important as I know they are. I have forced myself to view a few, including *Schindler's List* and *The Pianist*, which I found to be exceptional, but those were difficult experiences for me. My aversion to viewing violence, moreover, has discouraged me from volunteering at the U.S. Holocaust Memorial Museum in Washington, an institution I admire immensely and whose importance I understand well. I know other child survivors who volunteer there weekly, most of them fellow members of "Survivors of the Holocaust—The Last Generation." Nobody, of course, needs to tell me how critical it is to keep the memory of the Holocaust alive, especially among the young. That is, after all, why I have written this work and why I periodically have given speeches at schools. But I have not been able to get myself to spend entire days at the museum, on a regular basis, surrounded by the horrors of the Holocaust. I simply have lived with too much of that.

110

Chapter 8. Falling for a Litvak

Perhaps not surprisingly, another of my worries has been that I might inflict too much of the Holocaust's psychological burdens on my own children and grandchildren, an issue I have discussed over the years with Noel. It is no secret that many children of survivors live difficult emotional lives, absorbing the anxieties of their emotionally scarred parents, their compulsive fears of injury and death, their endless sense of mourning for the departed, their outbursts under stress and their excessive expectations for children's success to help make up for all that was lost. This is by no means the case with all survivors' children; many have been found to be no more or less affected than other children by their parents' histories. As Elie Wiesel told the First International Conference of Children of Holocaust Survivors in 1984, "The great majority of you remain healthy and generous, with a sense of humor, with a sense of literature and culture and humanity. That you are so well-adjusted seems almost abnormal." My hope was that our children and grandchildren would fall into this abnormally normal group, and that seems to have been the case, at least for the most part.

Our daughter Stephanie, for example, has long been driven to succeed, attending prestigious universities and creating and managing her own government-relations and public policy firm in Washington. But this cannot be attributed to any pressures on her stemming from my Holocaust experience. On the contrary, as she will tell you, "What I valued most was the survival part" of our Holocaust history. "It made me feel as if I could do almost anything." As for any other Holocaust links to her behavior, she says, "It's messy, hard to single out" from other factors in her life.

Our younger daughter, Pamela, who lives outside Chicago, was different. As she will tell you, for a time during her teenage years she suffered from "anxieties about death and loss" and experienced "a lot of nervousness about getting hurt. If I just skinned my knee I felt like the world was tumbling down." In fact, for a brief period she even refused to venture outside the house. All this, however,

Part III. The New World

cannot simply be ascribed to growing up amid tales of Holocaust horrors. In fact, her intense worries were triggered by witnessing a terrible accident in which a high school classmate dove into the shallow end of a pool, damaged his cervical spine, and became a quadriplegic. After that trauma, it was difficult for her to be at school for several months. During the therapy that I arranged for her during this period, her discussions naturally covered the Holocaust as well as her classmate's accident. Ultimately, Pam, who also attended exceptional universities, studied psychology and focused professionally on aiding emotionally troubled juveniles and their families.

As for Stephanie's two daughters and Pam's three sons, I have not been able to detect any signs that our family's Holocaust history has damaged the grandchildren's lives.

Chapter 9
Debts

A promise made is a debt unpaid.

—*Robert W. Service*

For many years a sense of debt has hovered over my family, and we have sought to meet our obligations as best we could. My mother, for example, regularly sent food, clothing and what money we could afford to Zofia Sendler in Poland. Initially we were not sure that the packages would reach her behind the Iron Curtain, but then she wrote to my mother that she had indeed received the first one. The packages, of course, were nothing like the substantial reward Zofia had been offered when she hid me, but they nonetheless made a difference in the Sendlers' lives, as Zofia told us when my mother and I visited her in Poland in August of 1985.

For me that was an eye-opening and tear-filled trip: I finally met with and spoke with the family that had hidden me, and I visited the country and city where I had been born. Poland generally was a dreary place in those Communist days—few cars, buildings in need of repair, shops with few goods, prices remarkably low. The hotels where we stayed in Warsaw and Krakow (in Krakow it was the Francuski, which my mother told me had once been elegant and expensive) cost little. Breakfast for two was less than $2, and a three-course dinner for both of us cost about $6. Getting our hair washed

113

Part III. The New World

and blow-dried ran about $1.50. (My mother gave the beautician a $2 tip, almost bowling her over.)

At the start of our trip, after our plane landed in Warsaw and we went to our hotel, we negotiated with drivers outside and chose one who charged $100 to take us around for a week, or less than $15 a day. After we spent part of a day visiting Warsaw sites—particularly the boundary markers where the Warsaw Ghetto once stood and the Nozyk Synagogue, the sole surviving prewar Jewish house of worship, which the Nazis had used as a stable—he drove nearly four hours to the Hotel Francuski in Krakow, where Zofia came to see us. We all cried and hugged and talked about our families. Then and later Zofia told me things I had not known before: that she had breast-fed me along with her daughter Danuta, who to this day calls me *moja siostra mleka* (my milk sister), and that the church where she had me baptized became one of the Krakow parishes of Father Karol Wojtyla, the future Pope John Paul II. She also told me how I had screamed when my mother came to take me away after the war.

The next day my mother showed me Krakow landmarks—the *Rynek Glowny*, the largest square of any Medieval city in Europe (and chosen, in 2005, as the world's best square); the old Jewish quarter of Kazimierz; a plaque marking the former Krakow Ghetto, where I was born; *Plac Zgody*, where Jews assembled during "selections" before being shipped to Belzec or Auschwitz or Treblinka. We also visited the large Künstler family home at Ujejskiego Street 13, which was now an apartment building. We knocked at the door of the caretaker, who refused to let us in. As we turned to go, a lovely family that lived there—parents, grandparents and a small blond-haired boy—arrived at the building. When we explained why we were there, they kindly asked us to come up to their apartment for tea. Upstairs they asked my mother to tell them her wartime tale, and when she did, their tears began flowing freely.

114

Chapter 9. Debts

The following day we met with Zofia Sendler's entire family, and we all hugged and told more stories and cried again. Red-eyed, Zofia told my mother that it would be helpful if in the future she sent dollars rather than goods, though she did ask us to mail one last item: material for a wedding dress for one of her granddaughters. We of course sent the material as well as a wedding veil, and my mother also gave Zofia extra money before we left.

After our three memorable days in Krakow, our driver took us to the Carpathians, to my mother's hometown of Zawoja, a small resort area with distinctive wooden architecture. Zawoje evolved into a resort because it is near *Babia Góra* (Old Wives' mountain), which can be seen from the road when you drive into town and which was dear to my nature-loving mother. Unsure how to find her childhood home after all those years, my mother had the driver stop by a house where an elderly man was painting a faded fence. She asked him if he knew where the Düklers had lived. He squinted at her with an expression of disbelief. "E-d-ja? Is that really you?" he said in Polish. He was a childhood friend, one of many she had had who were not Jewish. Excited, he embraced her, tears in his eyes, and gave the driver directions to the home of my mother's youth. As we were approaching that old house, three women who were working in a nearby farm field—still swinging scythes—came running down to us, shouting, "Edja! Edja!" Also friends from my mother's youth, they quickly had gotten word that "Eda Dükler is in Zawoja." They were beside themselves with joy, gushing, telling my mother how ecstatic they were that she had survived, that they could speak with her again. More stories and tears flowed, especially when the friends described how the bodies of my grandparents and my mother's youngest sister had been thrown into a mass grave after the Nazis shot them. Later, we were told, a gravestone had been placed at the spot, and it had been consecrated by the reading of a Jewish prayer (no doubt the mourner's *Kaddish*). When we went to look for the stone, however, it was gone. We asked what had happened and were informed that because of

115

Part III. The New World

a shortage of building materials, the stone had been stolen. It evidently was used as part of somebody's house.

At her childhood home—a simple wooden structure with steps leading to a wooden porch from which you could enter either the house or, adjacent to it, my grandparents' general store—my mother behaved as if she were a teenager again, hurrying up and down steps, inspecting the rooms and the store, excitement in her voice. The store, she said, also had served as a synagogue for the tiny Jewish community of Zawoja, with a prized Torah taken out for *Shabbat* and the high holidays. The house had no indoor bathroom, only an outhouse in the back. Also, down an incline, which had stone steps, was a creek that was beloved by my mother, who said that she would picnic or read beside it in warm weather. The house was scheduled to be demolished and replaced by a more modern dwelling, we were told. My mother was pleased that I had gotten to see it before it was destroyed.

From Zawoje we drove back to Warsaw—along the way encountering thousands of Catholics from that year's pilgrimage for the Black Madonna of Czestochowa, the most popular shrine in Poland—and then we flew back to the United States.

■ ■ ■

We tried to repay our debt to the Sendlers in other ways as well. Just months after our trip to Poland, in early 1986, my family had a visitor at our house in Silver Spring: Zofia's daughter Danuta. My mother had arranged for her to come to the United States for six months, getting her the necessary papers and sending her round-trip plane tickets. The intent was for Danuta to earn money here, save it, and take it back to Poland, part of a temporary workforce Poland was dispatching to various nations.

I knew absolutely nothing of this plan. I learned about it only from a phone call in which my mother told me that Danuta would

Chapter 9. Debts

soon arrive in New York—and that she was being sent down to me. Really? Why? Because my parents were leaving on vacation and therefore could not deal with her. Then why did my mother arrange for Danuta to come now? She had gotten her dates confused, my mother said, so I needed to take Danuta. But we had a small ranch house with little extra room, I reminded her. You'll figure it out, she said, and she'll be of help to you. Thus Danuta Sendler, who does not speak a word of English, came to Silver Spring, Maryland.

A large and strong woman, she was indeed of help shortly after she arrived. It snowed heavily one night, so in the morning I asked her in Polish if she would shovel our walkway. I may have mispronounced a word—my Polish was rusty—but when Danuta came back into the house she had shoveled not only our walkway but much of our street as well, doing the work normally left to plows. I was stunned, as were neighbors when I explained what had happened.

Danuta slept in our basement, which had a separate bathroom, and earned money mainly from housework, baby-sitting and senior care. She worked in my house two days a week in addition to doing some cooking (she seemed to have a compulsion to cook potato pancakes, which were made with too much oil for my family). She also babysat for the son of close friends a couple of afternoons a week, and she took care of an elderly parent for a couple who owned a Polish food store in Silver Spring on other days. She had met the couple at a Polish church in Silver Spring where I took her on Sundays.

Strangely, that church—Our Lady Queen of Poland / St. Maximilian Kolbe Parish–was connected to my life in several ways. First, "Our Lady Queen of Poland" honors the Virgin Mary, and the church contains an icon of the Black Madonna of Czestochowa, who was named Queen of Poland in 1656. Thus, it was a reminder of the pilgrimage that my mother and I encountered in Poland and in which we briefly participated.

117

Part III. The New World

Second, St. Maximilian Kolbe, the church's co-patron, is known as "the saint of Auschwitz." That is because he volunteered to die in Auschwitz in place of a condemned Polish officer. The Nazis thus murdered Kolbe at age 47, injecting carbolic acid into his veins after he had spent weeks in a starvation chamber (the stranger he saved lived until the age of 93). Kolbe, it should be said, has a good number of critics, and for good reason: his history of anti-Semitic writings, including some works echoing the Jewish conspiracy theory at the heart of the *Protocols of the Learned Elders of Zion*, the fictitious nonsense that was widely believed in his day. But it is also important to note that in his friary outside Warsaw, Kolbe protected many Jews (accounts of the number range from several hundred to more than 2,000) as well as others from the Nazis before he ended up in Auschwitz for doing so.

Finally, it was the future Pope John Paul II—when he visited the United States in 1969 and 1977 as Archbishop Karol Wojtyla of Krakow—who raised the question of a church for Polish Catholics to worship in the Washington, D.C., area. A stone church near my house that had been completed in 1894, Silver Spring's old St. John's, ultimately was chosen as the site, and St. Maximilian Kolbe, whose life's work was devoted to the Virgin Mary, became the church's co-patron after Pope John Paul II canonized him in 1982. The church became a parish in 1983, just three years before Danuta came to stay with us. She felt at home there, especially since Sunday mass and holy day services were conducted in Polish.

Indeed, Danuta was happy in general. She had almost no expenses and thus saved her money, at least until she had enough to buy things. She could not seem to get her fill of shopping, often walking to the supermarket or to the now-defunct Hecht's department store in downtown Silver Spring to purchase something for herself or her children. Periodically, I sent packages back to Poland for her. She was so happy, in fact, that she told me that she wanted to stay with us for a year, not six months.

118

Chapter 9. Debts

I didn't oppose that, in part because I was preoccupied with family, work and another plan: a coming visit to Japan. I was among 50 Americans, Canadians and Europeans who had been selected to spend a month in Japan. We were to be guests of the government in a program sponsored by the Ministry of Trade and Industry (MITI).

Although I very much wanted to go, I debated for a while about whether to leave my family and my lobbying job for a month. My husband, however, encouraged me to do it, even though we had never been apart for that long and he was jealous that he could not go with me. He certainly was not looking forward to being left with Danuta; he was no fan of her oily potato pancakes, and he could not communicate with her beyond playing their daily version of Twenty Questions, using hand motions and pointing and physically showing her what he wanted. Stephanie, who had already graduated from college, was working in downtown Washington and living with a girlfriend in the District. Pam was all grown; she would graduate soon from high school and then spend several months in Israel with her Jewish Day School graduating class; she was pondering colleges, and my husband planned to take her on at least one campus trip while I was gone. He said that the timing seemed good for me to go and that it would be a mistake for me to pass up an opportunity to see and learn about Japan. When would I have another chance like this?

So I flew to Tokyo in September 1986. It was the heyday of "Japan Inc.," which was characterized by, among other things, the country's interlocking banking and business conglomerates, its MITI-managed industrial policies, its acquisitions of U.S. real estate and corporate assets, and an American fear that we might be eclipsed economically by The Rising Sun. Japan's economic bubble, of course, burst four years later, but in 1986 the Japanese felt like masters of the universe and wanted to "educate" the West about their cultural and economic model.

Part III. The New World

The program's lectures began in Tokyo, where U.S. Ambassador Mike Mansfield, Sony chairman Akio Morita and an array of professors spoke to us. Then we rode Japanese bullet trains and buses to other cities—Fujinomiya, Hamamatsu, Kyoto, Kobe, Nagoya, Osaka–and I lived briefly with a Japanese family. During the day we attended more briefings, learned elementary Japanese, and visited Honda, Toyota and Nissan plants and other facilities. In the evenings we usually enjoyed lavish dinners, conversation and karaoke. One day the program director asked me to hit golf balls with him. I told him that I had the worst eye-hand coordination of anyone in the Western world, but he insisted. So I kept swinging at the ball without hitting it, only digging divots in the turf. He finally believed me and said, "You make a great farmer."

All in all, it was a wonderful trip, and I learned much. But it was good to go home again.

Several months after I returned to Washington, Danuta left for Poland, her suitcases stuffed with American purchases. We continued to stay in touch regularly after that, but I did not see her again until 25 years later, when Noel and I went with Harvey and Helene to Poland in May of 2012. By then Danuta's mother, her father and two brothers had passed away. Danuta was the sole survivor, and she was having difficulties with her own family, financially and otherwise. I left her money and continue to send her more, but I cannot satisfy what she would really like to see happen: regaining my father's family house on Ujejskiego Street, presumably so she might receive a share of it. On the advice of a Washington friend—another child survivor who had succeeded in recovering prewar property in Poland—I retained a Krakow attorney to explore the issue. Unfortunately, after checking the building's prewar and postwar history in the city land and mortgage registry, she concluded that the property was, for several reasons, "unrecoverable." So the debt to the Sendlers will never be fully repaid.

120

Chapter 10

New York City Crisis and Beyond

"Help!"

> —*Note placed among the prayers in Jerusalem's*
> *Wailing Wall by former New York mayor*
> *Abraham Beame*

I was angry. Really angry. New York City, one of the glories of America, the city that had opened its arms to millions of immigrants, that educated us and nurtured us, that defined the possible in theater and finance and art and media and so much else, had become a verbal punching bag.

Recall, for example, President Gerald Ford's October 1975 rejection of New York's request for Washington to help the city out of a financial mess, prompting the famous *New York Daily News* headline: "FORD TO CITY: DROP DEAD." The President, of course, hadn't said that; he simply had refused to lift a finger to help New York avoid defaulting on its debt. In fact, he wanted to make it *easier* for the city to declare bankruptcy and vowed to veto any legislation designed to let it escape that fate. On top of that, Ford's wiseacre Treasury Secretary, William E. Simon, ridiculed the city, announcing: "We're going to sell New York to the Shah of Iran. It's a hell of an investment."

Mayor Beame's plea for divine intervention clearly wasn't working. The city consequently had to scramble on its own to avoid one near-disaster after another. It slashed its workforce, cut salaries of remaining workers, raised taxes, instituted new fees and

121

Part III. The New World

persuaded city unions to pony up pension funds for city coffers at critical junctures. Banks deferred payments and lowered interest on the New York debt that they held and bought long-term city bonds issued by a new state agency. Some foreign governments and other U.S. cities joined New York in pressing Washington to provide assistance, mainly out of fear of a financial calamity at home and abroad if the city did declare bankruptcy. Finally, the President relented, and in November a law was passed providing New York with up to $2.3 billion in short-term loans over three years and charging it 1% above the federal cost of borrowing money. The loans were approved on the condition that New York would put its fiscal house in order by the end of the three years so that it could borrow again on its own. But that did not happen.

With Ed Koch now mayor and Jimmy Carter in the White House, New York in 1978 still needed the federal government to guarantees its loans in order to have any credibility in municipal bond markets, and some Americans were not happy about that. I remember sitting in our living room after our daughters had gone to sleep and reading in the paper about Texans who reckoned that the best solution was for the rest of the country to "just let New York fall into the East River." That got my blood boiling. "I'd love to shove those Texans into a river!" I said. Then I blurted out: "Actually, I'd like to get all the Americans who grew up or went to school or worked in New York to give a couple of bucks to the city and solve the budget crisis once and for all. There must be millions of us!"

My husband looked up from a book he was reading and said, "I'm afraid that wouldn't solve anything even if you could do it. The city needs billions of dollars and has to replenish that regularly. If you want to help New York, you probably could accomplish much more by organizing those former New Yorkers and getting them to support the federal loan-guarantee bill that's in Congress now." Then he went back to reading.

Chapter 10. New York City Crisis and Beyond

I'm sure he didn't think I would take him seriously—but I did, at least seriously enough to explore the idea. I phoned some of my many friends in the Washington area who were from New York City and asked what they thought of the notion. I was surprised by how strongly they felt about doing it. They wanted to pay back the city for all it had done for us, to provide one answer to Abe Beame's "Help!" request. As a Holocaust survivor, I had particularly strong emotions about this: I felt that I had a deep debt to repay to the city that had opened its doors for us.

The problem was that I had never created or run an organization in my life, and I certainly had no experience in politics. My college degree was in speech therapy, and my first job was to research pronunciations for the unabridged Random House Dictionary of the English Language. After giving birth to our two daughters, I worked hard as mother and housewife for seven years before returning to college in the evenings to become a teacher of English to students of other languages, a career for which I had an obvious affinity. At the time of the New York fiscal crisis I was working at a school that prepared foreigners for the English exam they had to pass in order to attend U.S. colleges. To start the New York group would require leaving that job and my students. I would miss my times with them, particularly the humorous moments. I remember once, for example, when I was trying to teach past tense and asked what the class had eaten for dinner. A Vietnamese student said, "I ate fuck."

As a few students giggled, I said, slowly, "You mean you ate with a fork?"

"No, no," he said, "I ate fuck. Fuck." At that point the entire class started laughing. The students slapped their desks and chanted, "Fuck, fuck, fuck, fuck," which echoed through the halls of the school. Thankfully, one student then shouted that the Vietnamese young man was trying to say that he ate "pork." The Vietnamese student nodded, indicating that this was correct, and

Part III. The New World

I raised my arms for the chanting to stop. I ended up telling the student that he would be wise never to order pork in an American restaurant.

Leaving my teaching job also would require giving up our second income, which would cause some strains, especially since we were trying then to begin saving for college educations. If I started the New York organization, though, I simply could not see myself drawing a salary. Whatever money we raised would be needed for so many other things, and much of the work, in any case, would have to be done by volunteers. That, in fact, is what happened when "Ex-New Yorkers for New York" was created. We had, for example, an all-volunteer board of directors. It included, among others:

- Dana Trier, at the time a young tax attorney at the law firm of former Internal Revenue Service Commissioner Sheldon Cohen (Dana went on to become a partner at New York's Davis Polk, a professor at Georgetown University Law School, and a key Treasury tax official). Cohen assigned Dana to apply for an IRS tax exemption for Ex-New Yorkers for New York and not to charge us anything for the work. The tax exemption was needed to help attract individual donations, such as one we received from New York real estate tycoon Lewis Rudin, as well as to cover the modest Ex-New Yorkers membership fee.

- Chester E. (Checker) Finn, Jr., then on the staff of New York Senator Pat Moynihan (and later an assistant U.S. secretary of education and head of the Thomas B. Fordham Foundation). Finn had suggested the membership fee and a corresponding slogan: "For you, $4.98." The fee covered costs of a newsletter and mailings, a Post Office Box, events such as rallies, occasional travel and odds and ends.

- Richard J. Whelan, a former writer for *Time, Fortune* and *The Wall Street Journal* who authored, among other works, *The Founding Father: The Story of Joseph P. Kennedy* and, more to the point, *A City Destroying Itself: An Angry View of New York*, which had grown out of a *Fortune* article.

124

Chapter 10. New York City Crisis and Beyond

Similarly, the Rev. Timothy S. Healy, S.J., the president of Georgetown University, was quite generous toward us. Healy was an ex-New Yorker, born in Manhattan, who had been vice chancellor of the City University of New York before heading Georgetown and who became president of the New York Public Library after leaving Washington. During a lunch that he arranged at the elegant *1789* restaurant near campus (named for the year the university was founded), Healy offered free use of a large university hall to hold a rally for New York City. I was deeply appreciative. The rally, which was designed to help get attention for the group, attracted a good number of Washington notables. They naturally included such New York lawmakers as Senator Jacob Javits and Rep. Charles Rangle as well as eminent Washington economists, attorneys, journalists, lobbyists, congressional staff members, administration officials and many others who had grown up on the city's streets.

At the same time, I put my family to work. My husband was on the board of directors and took on an array of tasks. Stephanie, who was 13 years old when Ex-New Yorkers for New York was created, became its Treasurer. In the evening, after she finished her homework, she sat at our dining room table (which was also our boardroom table and newsletter table and general planning table) and opened mail and recorded checks, many of them in response to an ad we were lucky enough to get placed for free.

Stephanie, 9-year-old Pam and many others helped organize and manage the Georgetown rally, setting up the hall, preparing news releases, directing guests and working the lights. The rally hall, for example, was filled with New York street signs that Mayor Koch's office had presented to me, and we hung a large banner created by an artist friend named Karla Klevin. Also in the hall were the ingredients for making a New York "egg cream" (Fox's U-Bet chocolate syrup, bottles of seltzer, and milk) so that everyone could make their own. A good number of the sophisticated guests ended up arguing about the best way to make the drink as well as about the secrets

125

Part III. The New World

of the many street games one could play with a Spalding "pink ball." In addition there were big hot pretzels like those we used to buy off carts on New York's streets, bagels and cream cheese, coffee and soft drinks (including Dr. Brown's cream soda) and bunches of candies provided by a couple from New York who had a candy store in Maryland (Stephanie couldn't keep away from the chocolate licorice). Atop of this we gave out little brass "Big Apple" pins that everyone wore.

Some speeches were given—a couple by political celebrities and one by me in which I urged support for the New York loan guarantee bill—and a local TV station aired coverage of the rally that night. As a result, more ex-New Yorkers signed up, and Stephanie continued to record fresh checks. (A few weekends later I also arranged for a stickball game to be played on Washington streets, but that did not go as well: It ended prematurely when we broke a window in the old U.S. Department of Health, Education and Welfare building—now the Department of Health and Human Services—and, in true New York fashion, swiftly fled the scene.)

We also were eager to attract ex-New Yorkers living elsewhere across the nation, and we were fortunate to accomplish that through op-ed columns that were accepted by such papers as the *Miami Herald*, the *Chicago Tribune* and the *Detroit Free Press*. The *Washington Post*'s Colman McCarthy also wanted to write a column on our group. My husband was uncomfortable when Colman approached him at work about this (Noel wanted no conflicts of interest), and he made clear to Colman that he could not encourage him to write such an article. Colman nonetheless came to our house and interviewed me, and the column he wrote ran not just in the *Washington Post* but in the *St. Petersburg Times* and other papers as well.

As the organization grew, many members, especially in Washington, wanted to lobby lawmakers on the House and Senate banking committees, which had jurisdiction over the loan-guarantee bill. The tax-exempt status of Ex-New Yorkers for New

126

Chapter 10. New York City Crisis and Beyond

York, however, prevented the group from lobbying. Nonetheless, several dozen people who were determined to contact the Congress on New York's behalf volunteered to do that on their own, separate from the group. They particularly targeted a Montgomery County, Maryland, member of the House, Republican Representative Newton Steers, who served on the House banking committee. The volunteers made so many calls to Steers that they tied up his office phone lines for a day or two, and their efforts seemed to work: Steers opposed the loan-guarantee bill in subcommittee, abstained in the full committee and ended up voting for the measure on the House floor.

All this helped give our members credibility with others who were lobbying for the loan-guarantee bill—major New York investment banks and commercial banks, New York unions and real estate interests, city and state officials and others. We were invited to their weekly strategy sessions at the Hyatt Regency Hotel on Capitol Hill. At first we were not taken very seriously. When they went round the table at the start of my first meeting, everyone else gave impressive introductions—they were from Chase Manhattan or Morgan Guarantee or the teacher's union or the mayor's office— but when I said, "Anita Epstein of Ex-New Yorkers for New York," it prompted chuckles. However, as our group grew in Washington and across the country (if memory serves me we ended up with somewhere between 750 and 1,000 members) they started paying serious attention to us. Suddenly they were asking, "Can you help us with Florida? Texas? Ohio?" I kept reminding them that our organization could not lobby but that ex-New Yorkers in those states could do so individually if they wished—and a good number of them did.

In January 1978, when Ed Koch was inaugurated mayor of New York City, the *Daily News* had quoted a White House aide as saying that "a long-term loan or guarantee has almost no chance in Congress." Five months later, on June 9, the House of

127

Part III. The New World

Representative voted overwhelmingly to approve the New York City Loan Guarantee Act of 1978, and on July 27 the Senate passed the final version of that law. Ex-New Yorkers for New York obviously had played only a small part in this turnaround, but my ex-New Yorker friends and colleagues were rightly proud and I was invited to represent them at the August 8, 1978 presidential bill-signing ceremony at New York's City Hall. It was a gratifying experience, especially when I listened to President Jimmy Carter say that "this greatest of cities" was "still a cultural and artistic and financial and diplomatic capital—not just for the nation but for the entire world," and "a center of compassion as well."

The small part that our group had played had a big effect on my life. Afterward, I decided not to return to teaching. Instead, I landed a job as Director of Government Affairs for the nation's state boards of education, whose offices were near the Congress. As my husband drove me to my new office, I saw the dome of the U.S. Capitol ahead. It suddenly hit me: They were going to let a *greenah* (an immigrant) like me lobby members of Congress. I broke into tears. It was a long way from my secret birth in the Krakow ghetto, from being hidden from the Nazis while my parents went through hell, from being torn, screaming, from the family that protected me and then escaping with my mother to Germany. It was a long way from incurring slaps in Selb because I was a Jew and from living with frequent postwar nightmares and malnutrition and rickets. And it was a long way from playing "Hit the Rat" in the streets of Bedford-Stuyvesant, from sitting in a class for the "retarded" because of my limited command of English, from having darts thrown in my back in junior high school, and from being attacked by three boys on the steps of our brownstone. That I now would be lobbying in Congress, the White House and elsewhere seemed to me like another miracle.

I obviously wanted to make the journey easier for my children and grandchildren, and in most ways it certainly has been. But

128

Chapter 10. New York City Crisis and Beyond

I do not kid myself about the precarious position of Jews today. I do not mean to suggest that we are facing the prospect of another Holocaust, of a government systematically murdering millions of Jews. We are not. We live in a different world with different demographic trends, different technology, different weapons and different kinds of anti-Semitism, as is made eminently clear in a valuable book called "Not Your Father's Anti-Semitism: Hatred of Jews in the Twenty-First Century," edited by Michael Berenbaum. But we nonetheless are in trouble again. I fret, for example, about the anti-Semitism that has flared up (once more) at U.S. colleges, especially as our oldest grandchild proceeds through her college career. The best schools are also where hostility toward Jews has been most notable, where anti-Semitic groups have campaigned for divestment of Jewish assets, where they have staged rallies equating Gaza with concentration camps, attacked Israelis as "Nazis," waved placards proclaiming "Hitler was right!" and burned Israeli flags. The attackers do not seem to have lured other students to their cause—most college students continue to have little knowledge about or interest in Middle East affairs—but they evidently have shaken a good number of Jewish students. For example, 43 percent of Jewish college students surveyed in 2011 by the Institute for Jewish and Community Research reported that they witnessed or experienced anti-Semitism on campus, and 41 percent heard a professor in class make anti-Israel remarks.

Despite all this, anti-Semitism is relatively moderate in the United States. It is far worse abroad. In recent decades, for example, Jews in Europe generally have not feared so much for their safety that they have thought of emigrating. That is no longer the case, not after years of murders of Jews in France, including the 2014 terrorist killing of four Jewish men at a kosher market outside Paris, the 2014 killing of four at the Jewish Museum of Belgium in Brussels, and the many anti-Semitic rallies on European streets, the attacks on Jewish community centers and the defacing of Jewish cemeteries and

129

Part III. The New World

neighborhoods. Now, according to a 2013 survey by the European Union Agency for Fundamental Rights, nearly 30% of Jews there are considering emigrating, including 25% in Germany, 40 percent in Belgium, 46 percent in France and 48 percent in Hungary. That is scary, but it is not the only troubling finding. Many European Jews also feel the need to hide the fact that they are Jewish. The agency found that 68 percent of Jews surveyed said that they occasionally, frequently or always avoid "wearing, carrying or displaying things that might help people identify them as Jews," such as a Star of David or a kippah.

The European experience is one part of a global anti-Semitic wave, as illustrated by a 2014 survey of more than 100 nations conducted for the Anti-Defamation League. It found that 26 percent of those polled were anti-Semites, representing more than 1 billion people. These were respondents who answered "probably true" to six or more age-old stereotypes about Jews, including that Jews "are responsible for most of the world's wars" and that we wield too much power in business and finance and too much control over global affairs, the U.S. government and the media. (Sound familiar?) Interestingly, another of the stereotypes cited was that "Jews still talk too much about what happened to them in the Holocaust" (36 percent thought that this was probably true). Sorry, but the evidence suggests the opposite: that we do not talk enough about the Shoah, no matter how much "Holocaust fatigue" is thought to exist. The ADL survey found, after all, that nearly half of those interviewed—and especially the young—had never even heard of the Holocaust. Of those under 35 years old, for instance, only 48 percent were aware of the Shoah. This can only reinforce worries that the world will pay less and less heed in the future to pleas from survivors like my mother who, after all the unspeakable horrors they endured, urged us "Not to forget." We cannot let them down. We cannot let their lives and deaths fade from the world's conscience, lest the world's conscience itself fade as well.

In Selb holding Peter's cat,
at about 4 years old.

Holding hands with Peter,
with his bunny on the ground
in front of us.

Picking flowers with a friend in Selb.

Standing in front of a DP who was leaving Selb in 1948 to fight in Israel's War of Independence. At left is my future father, Romek Kaminski, who is next to his sister, Fela; behind Fela is her husband Henik with their son Paul. To the left of the Israel-bound DP is Romek's other sister, Manya, with daughter Inka and husband Monyek.

My luggage tag from the USAT Harry Taylor when we finally made it to New York in November 1949.

Photo taken in 1957 when I was auditioned for the part of Anne Frank in the 1959 George Stevens film.

Used by permission of 20th Century Fox.

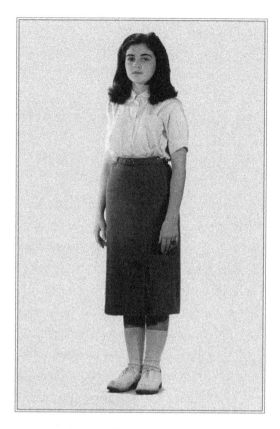

The Avalon Theater in Brooklyn, depicted on the very weekend I met my future husband there.

Century's Avalon Theatre, 1961, v1974, 9.349; John D. Morrell photographs, ARC.005; Brooklyn Historical Society

Afterword

I clearly have lived a full life so far, and now I have had a chance to give testimony about what happened to me and others during the Holocaust and afterward. While this does not remove all the pain I feel, putting it all down does provide an important sense of a burden at least partially lifted. But there is one final issue that I still need to confront, because when the Shoah Foundation interviewer asked my mother what she would say to her children and grandchildren, my mother did not merely reply, "Not to forget." She also gave a second answer: "Not to forgive."

I have long thought about this request, especially as Jews in the United States and Israel have appeared to become more and more accepting of the Germans. That has not been easy for me to watch. My mother, however, need not have worried about me on this score. I will never forgive the murderers or their descendants, as I made clear in an article that I published in the online *Jewish Daily Forward*.*

The article, which also appeared in Israel's *Haaretz* and elsewhere, prompted a good number of responses, most of them attacks on me. It did not surprise me that many disapproved of my view. Humanity has spent centuries, after all, stressing the importance of forgiveness, as reflected in texts from the world's religions, pronunciations of literary lions, and volumes from

---

* "Why I Cannot Forgive Germany," *Jewish Daily Forward*, June 9, 2010, adapted here with permission.

134

Afterword

modern psychology and psychiatry. You will not find comparable works on, say, "The Joy of Sticking It to Them" or "The Pleasure of Watching Them Squirm." For me and for a number of other Holocaust victims of my acquaintance, however, arguments of the forgiveness faction generally miss the mark. Consider perhaps the most well-worn dictum in favor of letting bygones be bygones: Alexander Pope's "To err is human, to forgive, divine." In my case I find it easily dismissible. This is not only because it would be disgraceful to apply a remark about literary criticism—the line is from Pope's 1711 "An Essay on Criticism," which is actually a poem—to Germany's systematic extermination of 6 million Jews. Even more, it would be outrageous to characterize so immense an abomination as "erring."

I am similarly unpersuaded by those who urge forgiveness because it can make those who do the forgiving feel better themselves. That's a favorite of psychiatrists and others dedicated professionally to making patients feel good. Thus, one can find works about how bestowing forgiveness can lift a weight from your shoulders, bring you peace, and improve your health in the process. The problem is that I have long felt tolerably well about myself. Indeed, for me the idea of forgiving Germans would have the opposite effect: It would make it hard for me to live with myself, to get out of bed in the morning and look in the mirror. I simply could not dishonor the memory of my many family members and the millions of other Holocaust victims by giving a free pass to the murderers and their progeny.

True, many have followed the forgiveness route and benefited. One of the most dramatic examples was Eva Kor, who, with her twin sister Miriam, was a victim of Dr. Josef Mengele's vile "experiments" on Jewish and Romani twins, dwarfs and others at Auschwitz. The subject of a documentary film called *Forgiving Dr. Mengele*, Kor stood before Auschwitz in the winter of 1995, 50 years after its liberation, and declared that she was granting

135

Afterword

"amnesty to all Nazis who participated directly or indirectly in the murder of my family and millions of others," including Mengele.

This took the Jewish community aback and infuriated other twins who had been Mengele victims. It will be recalled, after all, that the "Angel of Death," as Mengele was known, had brutalized and killed thousands. He selected twins for experiments on heredity, on relationships between racial types and disease, on eye coloration and on other questions posed by his mentor in Berlin. Mengele put children through excruciating pain, ordering surgeries, spinal taps and other procedures without anesthesia. He had some twins infected with deadly diseases, others castrated, still others injected in the eye with chemicals, and at least one set of twins sewn together. Many twins were killed with injections of phenol or chloroform into their hearts, after which their eyes and other organs were sent to Berlin for examination. That is the man Kor wanted to forgive.

Whether she knew it or not, however, Kor had her own Jewish problem: Judaism did not give her the ability to forgive Mengele or others. Judaic paths to forgiveness are unlike those of other religions. In Judaism, for example, one does not ask God's forgiveness for wrongs one commits again other people, only for sins committed against God. For sins against others, Jewish law and tradition require the offenders to express remorse, genuinely repent, provide recompense to victims if appropriate—and *ask* the victim for forgiveness. Only then can the victims forgive them. Obviously, Josef Mengele did not repent or ask Kor or other victims for forgiveness. So as far as Judaism is concerned, then, she could not forgive him, and she surely could not speak for her family or other victims or forgive all other Nazis.

Because of Jewish doctrine regarding forgiveness, some Jewish and Christian scholars have been groping for some time with the question of whether, when all of Hitler's henchmen and their victims are gone, the Jewish community will have any ability to grant forgiveness for the Holocaust. The answer seems to be that

136

Afterword

it will not. For me, though, this was not a terribly difficult question to begin with: I believe that the Holocaust is among what Moses Maimonides, in his *Mishneh Torah*, the twelfth-century compilation of Jewish religious law, suggested were sins so hideous as to be beyond the realm of human forgiveness.

Like anybody else, of course, Kor could come to terms personally with the atrocities committed by Mengele and others. While that certainly would not absolve Mengele or other Nazis of their sins, it could—and evidently did—help Kor. "I felt a burden of pain was lifted from me," she said. "I was no longer in the grip of pain and hate; I was finally free. The day I forgave the Nazis, privately I forgave my parents whom I hated all my life for not having saved me from Auschwitz. Children expect their parents to protect them, mine couldn't. And then I forgave myself for hating my parents. Forgiveness is really nothing more than an act of self-healing and self-empowerment."

I'm afraid not. Forgiveness is, by definition, much more than a self-centered act. What Kor is describing is closer to catharsis, a purging of pain, a very different process—and one that not all Holocaust survivors wish to experience. The late Elie Wiesel, for example, once remarked, "I want to keep that pain; that zone of pain must stay inside me." While I did not suffer from the unspeakable horror of the concentration camps as Wiesel, my mother, some of my murdered family members, Kor and so many others did, I know what he means. I, too, want to hold onto my pain. It helps ensure that the past is always present in me. It is an important part of what keeps me close to those I lost and to the world that died with them.

The pain also helps me deal with other questions, particularly whether Germans who were small children during World War II or who were born after the Holocaust—meaning the majority of today's Germans—should share guilt for the actions (or inactions) of their parents and grandparents. I have close family members and good friends who feel, quite strongly, that they should not, and

Afterword

I have been taken to task by others as well for holding an opposing view. One critic who responded to my *Forward* article, for example, said that I did not "understand the Judaic teachings—never to blame nor (*sic*) punish the sons and daughters for the sins of their fathers." For him and others I would note a passage in the Torah in which Moses is pleading his case to God: "The LORD is slow to anger, abounding in love and forgiving sin and rebellion. Yet He does not leave the guilty unpunished; he punishes the children for the sin of the father to the third and fourth generation" (Numbers 14:18). Similar language about punishing the children to the third and fourth generation for the sins of the father can be found elsewhere in the Torah as well (see Exodus 34:7 and Deuteronomy 5:9).

I am mindful of interpretations of these verses that exclude the innocent in succeeding generations from suffering, and I appreciate the generous nature of those who favor forgiveness for the children and grandchildren. Such opinions, however, usually are held by people who did not endure or witness the suffering of the Holocaust, people who are a generation or two removed from the horrors. I think that such people, good-hearted though they may be, may find that the answer is not as simple as they think. A good number of them, after all, probably are among those who insist on collective guilt for atrocious episodes in America's past— the horrors of slavery, the slaughter of Native Americans, the World War II internment of Japanese Americans and other acts committed in our name. Such American guilt has been passed from generation to generation (though our forebears were in many cases not even on these shores when the events occurred), and it has spawned such contemporary public responses as affirmative action, Japanese-American reparations payments and compensatory education.

Like a number of other nations, today's Germany also struggles with collective guilt for the sins of parents and grandparents. Germany's burden is especially heavy, because it stems from what former German chancellor Gerhard Schröder rightly termed

Afterword

"the greatest crime in the history of mankind," the ultimate sin. Nations cannot easily shed that kind of guilt, and certainly not in a generation or two.

It scarcely needs saying that this is why Germany today still tries so hard to make amends with the Jewish community. It not only has made restitution payments for more than 70 years and continues to do so to the dwindling number of Holocaust survivors. It also is a staunch supporter of Israel in Middle East controversies and is Israel's second-largest trading partner. It has encouraged the renewal of a sizable Jewish community in Germany. It has built Holocaust memorials, created Holocaust school curricula, maintained former concentration camps as museums. This is as it should be. If the pain of the past is always present in me, as it is in many other survivors and their children, it does not trouble me that contemporary Germans live with pain from that past as well. After all, just as children inherit genes and wealth and benefit from their parents' achievements, so do they inherit their parents' debts, including this one.

Many in the American Jewish community are understandably eager to respond to Germany's gestures toward the Jewish community and Israel, as well as to public statements of remorse by Protestant and Catholic leaders for the mistreatment of Jews. I surely endorse reconciliation with Christian communities in general. I also understand the importance of Jewish and Israeli links to Germany today, just as I understand how U.S. national interests dictated that America's main World War II enemies, Germany and Japan, became our postwar allies or that today we have shifting alliances with former foes like Russia and China. Such is the world of *realpolitik*.

On a personal level, however, I feel quite differently. While I am mindful of how many Jews in Germany today are from the former Soviet Union, I still find it hard to comprehend why any Jew would

Afterword

want to live in that country. What is even more difficult for me to deal with is that in recent years thousands of younger Israeli Jews have been moving to Berlin. Their historic memory evidently has been so weakened that they can be lured away by economic and cultural baubles or by the illusion that German anti-Semitism is not as bad as many believe. As for myself, I can never again set foot on German soil. I flinch when I even hear a conversation in German, the language I spoke when I first arrived in the United States at 7 years old.

In short, there are obvious strategic and practical reasons for reconciling and dealing with Germany. None, however, would move me to forgive all Germans today for the horrors of the Holocaust even if I had the ability to do so. In the end, I think, Germans will have to ask the Almighty for such absolution (though I sure would like to be there during those conversations).